I found myself nodding, underlining, and r ... page. *Jesus Journey* has a vitally important n ... passionate, Trent Sheppard exposes our dual ... liberates our deepest humanity. This book has the power to reintroduce you to the one you always longed to know.

—PETE GREIG, 24-7 Prayer and Emmaus Road

In this immersive experience of a book, Jesus' life leaps right off the page and into our lives with disruption and hope and healing. *Jesus Journey* reminded me of not only why I follow Jesus but why I love him so.

—SARAH BESSEY, author, *Jesus Feminist* and *Out of Sorts: Making Peace with an Evolving Faith*

Trent Sheppard's new book, *Jesus Journey*, is a wonder. It's an invitation for both Christians and non-Christians to explore the incidents, people, and circumstances of Jesus' life to understand how they impact our lives today. Anyone interested in a well-grounded exploration of both the historical Jesus and the Christ of faith—for they are one and the same—can't find a better guide than this book.

—ROBERT J. HUTCHINSON, author, *The Dawn of Christianity* and *Searching for Jesus*

Like Paul commended Titus to the church in Corinth and Phoebe to the church in Rome, I commend my friend Trent Sheppard to you. Trent is the real deal. He's taught multitudes, and his mind "runs deep" with the things of God. His message will inform, inspire, and ignite your walk with Jesus. Read and be blessed!

—LOREN CUNNINGHAM, founder, Youth With A Mission

Read this book and see Jesus from new angles; he lives on its pages. Trent Sheppard brings us into the wonderfully unsettling place of drawing near and seeing Jesus more clearly.

—THE REVEREND TIMOTHY CLAYTON, Rector of Christ the Redeemer Anglican Church on Boston's North Shore; author, *Exploring Advent with Luke*

My good friend and kingdom-coconspirator Trent has authority in painting a portrait of Jesus because he's fought so hard to stay right on his heels. I want to see and know the man I have given my life to following, and *Jesus Journey* adds a beautiful brushstroke to my portrait of the real, raw, relatable, freckled, passionate, all-powerful King Jesus. I will joyfully never see him the same.

—BRAD CORRIGAN, member of the indie band Dispatch; founder and president, Love Light & Melody

In a time when the church is waking up to our call to image God to the world, this book is a gift. Through brilliant storytelling and without compromising the divinity of Jesus, Trent brings the reader face to face with this unique, compelling, Jewish man from Nazareth. Be prepared to gaze upon Jesus in ways that will change you forever.

—MAUREEN MENARD, Director of Christian Formation and
Discipleship, University of the Nations, Youth With A Mission

Jesus Journey opened the eyes of my heart to see the "Word who became flesh" like never before. It's such a tragedy that we can become so familiar with Jesus' story that we miss the majesty and wonder of who he truly is. *Jesus Journey* took my heart on a journey from familiar to fascinated. This is the kind of book that goes beyond just filling your head with information; it leads your heart into an encounter with the real and living God.

—JONATHAN HELSER, singer-songwriter
of the viral hit "No Longer Slaves"

Jesus is and always will be the greatest leader the world has ever seen, and Trent explores the practical, faith-in-action elements of Jesus' life and humanity that should inspire each of us to go and make an impact in our communities. Jesus is the transformer of lives, and *Jesus Journey* shows us what it practically means to follow him in a deeper way.

—BRAD LOMENICK, former president, Catalyst;
author, *H3 Leadership* and *The Catalyst Leader*

In an age of division within the church and tension with the world, Trent Sheppard draws us back to the compelling personality and beautiful humanity of Jesus. Beyond being a beloved campus minister, Trent Sheppard is a theologian rich in profound godly insight. While reading, I recalled my first love for Christ. After reading, I love him more. A gift to the church and the world.

—KELLY MONROE KULLBERG, coauthor and editor,
Finding God at Harvard; founder, The Veritas Forum

Here is iconoclasm: recovering the real Jesus out of religious iconography.

—VISHAL MANGALWADI, author,
The Book That Made Your World

JESUS JOURNEY

Shattering the Stained Glass
Superhero and Discovering
the Humanity of God

Trent Sheppard

 ZONDERVAN®

ZONDERVAN

Jesus Journey
Copyright © 2017 by Trent Sheppard

Requests for information should be addressed to:
Zondervan, 3900 *Sparks Dr. SE, Grand Rapids, Michigan 49546*

ISBN 978-0-310-34776-7 (softcover)

ISBN 978-0-310-34772-9 (ebook)

Unless otherwise marked, Old Testament quotations are from New Revised Standard Version Bible. Copyright © 1989 National Council of the Churches of Christ in the United States of America. Used by permission. All rights reserved.

Unless otherwise marked, New Testament quotations are from *The Kingdom New Testament: A Contemporary Translation* by N. T. Wright. Copyright © 2011 by Nicholas Thomas Wright. Reprinted by permission of HarperCollins Publishers.

Scripture quotations marked *The Message* are from *The Message*. Copyright © by Eugene H. Peterson 1993, 1994, 1995, 1996, 2000, 2001, 2002. Used by permission of Tyndale House Publishers, Inc.

Any Internet addresses (websites, blogs, etc.) and telephone numbers in this book are offered as a resource. They are not intended in any way to be or imply an endorsement by Zondervan, nor does Zondervan vouch for the content of these sites and numbers for the life of this book.

Cover design: *Charles Brock | Faceout Studio*
Cover photo: © *Zwiebackesser / Shutterstock®*
Interior design: *Kait Lamphere*

First printing December 2016 / Printed in the United States of America

For Bronwyn
and
Miréa, Blaze, and Petra

Religion without humanity is very poor human stuff.

—SOJOURNER TRUTH (1797–1883)

CONTENTS

AUTHOR'S NOTE

Did you know that Saint Nicholas (yes, that St. Nick) once punched a guy? According to tradition, it all went down at the Council of Nicaea in AD 325.

Church bishops were gathered from all over the empire. One of the main reasons they were in Nicaea was to discuss the nature of Jesus' divinity. A popular and increasingly influential teacher named Arius was claiming that Jesus had been created by the Father, and Jesus the Son was lesser than and not equal to God.

But old St. Nick wasn't having any of it.

In a fit of fury that flies in the face of our cherished images of Santa Claus, Saint Nicholas became so irate during the debate that he lost his cool and smacked Arius in the face. (Talk about the Santa I never knew.)

While I strongly disagree with St. Nick's methodology—settling a debate with violence—I do agree with his conclusion: that Jesus, the Son of God, is one with and equal to the Father.

The reason I tell you this story about Saint Nicholas and Arius is to emphasize two critical points: (1) people of faith have been wrestling with and discussing the humanity and divinity of Jesus for a very long time, and (2) that discussion can get a little heated.

You see, talking about what is most dear to us is a vulnerable, heart-exposing journey—it can raise all sorts of issues inside, from anger to awe—and writing this book has certainly been that sort of journey for me.

I DECIDED TO WRITE *JESUS JOURNEY* BECAUSE I AM FASCI-nated with Jesus. More than anything else, it was fascination that informed my writing, shaped my approach, and urged me toward completion.

While my graduate work included a great deal of research in Christian history, most of my formal studies concentrated on people and movements of later eras, not specifically the first century. It wasn't until I completed my master's degree, about fifteen years ago, that I really began to immerse myself in a more thorough understanding of the world in which Jesus lived.

Whether it was the scholarly work of Anglican bishop and New Testament historian N. T. Wright, the insightful take of Rabbi Jacob Neusner, or the historical fiction of novelist Anne Rice, I just couldn't get enough of seeing Jesus in his historical setting.[1] His first-century words and ways, shrouded in mystery for so much of my life, were coming alive in a whole new way.

This wasn't just dusty, old history, the ivory-tower domain of pro-fessors and preachers. This was a doorway into another time, another world, a world in which this first-century teacher and healer had given us a glimpse of the face of God, and my faith, my hope, and, yes, even my love, were on fire.

To this day, Jesus is the most fascinating, brilliant, courageous, com-passionate, revolutionary, and compelling person I've ever encountered. If it really is true that we have seen the face of God in Jesus—and, oh God, I'm convinced it is!—well, then, that changes *everything*.

With that in mind, I write first as a devoted fellow pilgrim on the journey, as someone who has experienced new life in Jesus, the sort of life I desperately want to tell others about.

But I also write as a boots-on-the-ground minister, as someone who is very much concerned with and involved in the practical and down-to-earth task of how to make this Jesus life accessible to others. Having served for two decades now in various ministerial roles as a youth worker, a teaching pastor, and a college minister, I am more convinced than ever it's not enough simply to think interesting thoughts about Jesus.

No, our faith and following of him is meant to be lived, day in and day out: in the nitty-gritty of our nine-to-five lives, in the real-world dynamics of workplace and campus, in the real-life concerns of neighborhood and home, in how we interact with friends and family. That's why this book is filled with application points and written in a conversational, nonacademic style. Because the goal, always, is to put these things into practice and not just think about them.

TO MAKE THE STORY OF JESUS AS ACCESSIBLE AS POSSIBLE, when it comes to the New Testament, I've primarily used N. T. Wright's recent and very readable translation, *The Kingdom New Testament*, while periodically drawing from Eugene Peterson's *The Message* as well.[2] (Whenever *The Message* is used, I have notated it next to the scripture reference.) For Old Testament passages, I've relied exclusively on the New Revised Standard Version.

You'll also note that when it comes to the Holy Spirit, I occasionally drop the article and simply refer to Holy Spirit. The reason I do this is because I think it helps to remind us that Holy Spirit is a distinct and real person of the Trinity. Whereas the titles Father and Son can more naturally remain personal because we're familiar with father-son language, the Holy Spirit is at times unintentionally interpreted more as a distant and mysterious "it," but Holy Spirit, thanks be to God, is just as personal and real as the Father and the Son. Dropping the article is my way of keeping that vital truth in mind.

Finally, regardless of what happens with the publishing of *Jesus Journey*, I will never regret the months of immersion in the gospel accounts that accompanied its writing. Blaise Pascal, one of the inspirations for my son's name, said, "The last thing one discovers in composing a work is what to put first." Learning, teaching, and writing about Jesus is one of the supreme treasures of my life, made all the more precious by the beloved four who have given so much to make this book possible: Bronwyn, Miréa, Blaze, and Petra. This book is dedicated to them, my favorite part of being human.

—*Trent Sheppard, East Boston, September 2016*

My proposal is not that we know what the word "god" means, and manage somehow to fit Jesus into that. Instead, I suggest we think historically about a young Jew, possessed of a desperately risky, indeed apparently crazy, vocation, riding into Jerusalem in tears, denouncing the Temple, and dying on a Roman cross—and that we somehow allow our meaning for the word "god" to be re-centered around that point.

—N. T. WRIGHT

JESUS HAD AN AUNT

I believe the ancient creed:

> That Jesus is the only Son of God,
> eternally begotten of the Father,
> God from God, Light from Light,
> true God from true God,
> begotten, not made,
> of one being with the Father.
> Through him all things were made.
>
> For us and for our salvation,
> he came down from heaven,
> was incarnate of the Holy Spirit,
> born of the Virgin Mary, and was made man.
>
> For our sake he was crucified under Pontius Pilate;
> he suffered death and was buried.
>
> On the third day he rose again in accordance with the Scriptures;
> he ascended into heaven and is seated at the right hand of the Father.
>
> He will come again in glory to judge the living and the dead,
> and his kingdom will have no end.

Yes, I believe the creed.

All of it.

But—and this is where it gets a little risky for some—I also believe this:

- Jesus had a quick wit, he was occasionally laugh-out-loud funny, and he was sometimes sarcastic.
- Jesus had to learn how to do things (like measuring, math, and writing), and surely he made some mistakes along the way.
- Jesus came from an unusual family—don't we all?
- Jesus was gutsy, compassionate, perceptive, and wise, but he wasn't born into the full maturity of all these qualities. No, according to the scriptures, he grew in wisdom (Luke 2:52).
- Jesus was human, like you and me, and if the gospel is true, he still is.

That's what this book is all about.

I STILL RECALL THE MOMENT IT DAWNED ON ME THAT JESUS had an aunt, the extraordinary, unsettling, and restorative impact it had on my faith.

Honestly, even though it seems so obvious now (Well, of course, he had an aunt!), the thought hit me with such force I wasn't sure how to respond.

It was the gospel of John that took me there. I was reading about the crucifixion of Jesus, trying to get my head and heart around its weighty, cosmic significance. I had so many questions, but one stood out among the rest: Why?

Why, oh why, did the Son of God have to die?

Then, out of nowhere, it seemed, my mind was directed toward a new train of thought. The question of why faded, and in its place, glaring and unmistakable, was the question of who:

Who, exactly, was this God-man who died so long ago?

I knew the correct answer theologically: "Jesus is the only begotten Son of God." That part was pretty clear to me. (At least I thought it was.)

But what struck me was something different. It was something new and mysterious, something my eyes had glided over more times than I could count but for various reasons had never truly seen:

"Jesus's mother was standing beside his cross. So was her sister, Mary the wife of Clopas, with Mary Magdalene too" (John 19:25).

Just so you understand, the mother of Jesus I knew.

And Mary Magdalene, of course, I knew who she was too.

But who on earth was this other woman, described as the sister of Jesus' mother, mourning there at the foot of the cross?

And that's when it hit, a tremor that triggered a tectonic shift in my view of God: Jesus had an aunt.

Maybe it sounds absurd (and, to be honest, I'm no longer bothered if it does), but the reason that one thought struck me with such profound and unyielding force is that all at once Jesus became more real to me.

He wasn't a stained-glass superhero anymore: he was somebody's nephew.

He wasn't a theological argument to be won: he was somebody's nephew.

He wasn't a sacrificial system to accept, he wasn't a candidate's talking point, he wasn't a phantomlike figure floating through ancient history claiming to be God (whatever that word might mean to you):

No—a thousand times, *no!*—Jesus of Nazareth was somebody's nephew.

You see, even though I had been walking with God for years by that point, when I realized Jesus had an aunt, it felt like my journey with Jesus was just beginning.

I GREW UP IN THE CHURCH. MY FATHER WAS A SOUTHERN Baptist pastor. To this day he's still one of the most powerful preachers I've ever heard. Plus, he's got lots of silvery white hair and he sports a full beard. Think Southern Baptist Santa Claus with sky blue eyes and a warm smile—that's Dad.

Mom was a newspaper journalist and schoolteacher. She started the private high school where my sister and I were educated. (Our older brother was already in college by that point.) When I was eighteen, Mom learned she had cancer. She's a survivor, thank God. I cannot imagine what life would have been like without her.

My parents were Southern Baptists in the Deep South, but they did not fit the Southern Baptist mold. One of the reasons why is that in 1970, the Holy Spirit got hold of my dad—in a Southern Baptist seminary, of all places. It's a good thing, too, because that unexpected encounter with God saved my parents' marriage right when it was on the verge of breaking.

By the time I came around, Mom and Dad had been walking with God for years. I can't remember a time when faith was not part of my life. It was just there, like oxygen, always.

Holding hands around the table and giving thanks before eating. Hearing stories from the Bible about Noah and King David, Mother Mary and Jesus. Sunday morning hymns and summertime service trips, Wednesday night prayer meetings and Christmastime youth camps.

Our family was so involved in the life of the church that my parents left me there by mistake one Sunday morning when I was about two years old.

Dad and Mom had driven to church in separate vehicles. After the service was over, they each assumed the other had taken me home. (To this day my older brother and sister claim they had no idea I was left behind. I don't buy it.)

When my parents arrived home and realized that neither of them had returned with two-year-old me, they made a mad drive back to the sanctuary, fearing the worst. Thankfully, though, they found me sitting quietly with the church elders, listening carefully and asking insightful questions about theology.

Well, not exactly.

I had fallen asleep on a padded pew, rolled to the ground without waking, and was still fast asleep on the plush, blue-carpeted floor when my parents found me at last.

YOU WOULDN'T THINK JESUS, OF ALL PEOPLE, WOULD EVER get left behind by his parents. Yet there's an unusual story in the gospel of Luke which recounts that scenario:

Every year Jesus' parents traveled to Jerusalem for the Feast of Passover. When he was twelve years old, they went up as they always did for the Feast. When it was over and they left for home, the child Jesus stayed behind in Jerusalem, but his parents didn't know it. Thinking he was somewhere in the company of pilgrims, they journeyed for a whole day and then began looking for him among relatives and neighbors. When they didn't find him, they went back to Jerusalem looking for him.

The next day they found him in the Temple seated among the teachers, listening to them and asking questions. The teachers were all quite taken with him, impressed with the sharpness of his answers. But his parents were not impressed; they were upset and hurt.

His mother said, "Young man, why have you done this to us? Your father and I have been half out of our minds looking for you."

He said, "Why were you looking for me? Didn't you know that I had to be here, dealing with the things of my Father?" But they had no idea what he was talking about.

So he went back to Nazareth with them, and lived obediently with them. His mother held these things dearly, deep within herself. And Jesus matured, growing up in both body and spirit, blessed by both God and people. (Luke 2:41–52 *The Message*)

Perhaps I am stretching the similarities between Jesus and me (which my enduring wife tells me I am prone to do), but my own experience of being left behind at church helped me to relate to Jesus' experience of being left behind at the Temple in a fresh and surprising way.

For starters, it helped me realize that parents—even the best ones—really could do something as preposterous as unintentionally leaving a child behind at the Temple. (Don't worry, Mom and Dad, all is forgiven!) This is especially true when you take into account that Jewish families in the first century made their annual pilgrimage to Jerusalem as an extended clan, including uncles and aunts, sisters and brothers, cousins and friends.

Next, it helped me to better appreciate the panic with which Jesus' parents returned to the Temple in search of him. "Young man, why have you done this to us?" his exasperated parents are recorded as saying. "Your father and I have been half out of our minds looking for you." Now that I am a parent myself, I can imagine the rush of relief and frustration I would feel if I were in a similar situation.

Finally, as I delved more deeply into this peculiar account—peculiar especially considering the unusual way the story wraps up, with Mother Mary "pondering these things in her heart" and the boy Jesus "growing in wisdom and in stature, and in favor with God and people" (as most translations read)—it struck me that this extraordinary story is the only glimpse the gospel writers provide into Jesus' childhood.

Why is that?

The answer that makes the most sense historically is this: There were no other extraordinary stories to tell. Young Jesus of Nazareth, for the most part, was like all the other kids.

And that got me to thinking: Let's say Jesus is a ten-year-old boy in small-town, ancient Nazareth and he's taking a math test. Does he get all the answers correct?

If he does get all the answers correct, is that because Jesus in some mysterious way "leans into" his "godness" (and would that be cheating?), or is it simply because he is a good student?

On the other hand, if ten-year-old Jesus does not get every answer correct on his math test (because, who knows, maybe math isn't his strongest subject?), does that take away from whom Jesus is?

THE CHURCH HAS HAD A VERY INTERESTING JOURNEY WITH the humanity of Jesus. To better understand that journey and to better understand why the implications of his humanity are so important for us now, it is probably wisest to begin with those who knew Jesus best, his friends and followers from the first century.

According to the gospel, Jesus' twelve disciples were an eclectic crew that included a number of blue-collar fishermen, a well-connected tax collector, a politically minded zealot, and a few more unlikely characters. Of these twelve, more stories are told of Simon Peter the Fisherman than of any other, and in one of those stories we gain insight into how Peter and Jesus related:

> Jesus and his disciples came to the villages of Caesarea Philippi. On the way he asked his disciples, "Who are people saying that I am?"
>
> "John the Baptist," they said, "or, some say, Elijah. Or, others say, one of the prophets."
>
> "What about you?" asked Jesus. "Who do you say I am?"
>
> Peter spoke up. "You're the Messiah," he said.
>
> He gave them strict orders not to tell anyone about him.
>
> Jesus now began to teach them something new.
>
> "There's big trouble in store for the son of man," he said. "The elders, the chief priests, and the scribes are going to reject him. He will be killed—and after three days he'll be raised." He said all of this quite explicitly.
>
> At this, Peter took him aside and started to scold him. But he turned around, saw the disciples, and scolded Peter.
>
> "Get behind me, Accuser!" he said. "You're thinking human thoughts, not God thoughts." (Mark 8:27–33)

While so much could be said about this passage, there are two essential points to note for our purposes. First, for the disciples, the title of Messiah, more than anything else, meant something like "coming, conquering king," a king who would raise an army, defeat the occupying Romans, restore the Jewish Temple, and rule over all, and this king, mind you, was certainly not supposed to die. He was supposed to reign.

Second, the title of Messiah—and this is important—definitely did not mean the same thing as *God* or *second person of the Trinity* to the disciples at this time.

How do we know that?

At least as it relates to the story, one need only observe that after identifying Jesus as the Messiah (or as the Christ, in Greek), Peter takes Jesus aside to "scold" him—or, in other translations, to "rebuke" him.

If at this point in the gospel account Peter believes Jesus is God, it is practically inconceivable that as a devout, God-fearing, first-century Jew, Peter would have taken Jesus aside to scold or rebuke him. It just doesn't make any historical sense.

That is not to say, though, that Peter and the others did not come to that mind-blowing, history-altering, Jesus-is-God conclusion in time—most fully after the resurrection and with the help of the Holy Spirit. The older I become, the more convinced I am it is only through the help of Holy Spirit that any of us are convinced of the full identity of Jesus.

It is after their Master has been raised from the dead and the Holy Spirit has been poured out that the deeper, tectonic-shifting identity of Jesus truly dawns on the bewildered disciples. In Peter's second letter, written many years after the resurrection and addressed to those who never knew Jesus in the flesh, the old fisherman-apostle is said to have poignantly described his journey with Jesus like this: "We were eyewitnesses of his grandeur" (2 Peter 1:16).

The apostle Paul addresses a similar theme when he begins his letter to the Colossians with one of the earliest hymns about Jesus: "He is the image of God, the invisible one . . . For in him all the Fullness was glad to dwell" (1:15, 19).

Here again, in the letter to the Hebrews, Jesus is described as "the shining reflection of God's own glory, the precise expression of his own very being" (1:3).

And then in the famous prologue to John's gospel: "In the beginning was the Word, and the Word was with God, and the Word was God . . . And the Word became flesh and lived among us" (1:1, 14 NRSV).

Or, as Pastor Eugene Peterson renders it, "The Word became flesh and blood, and moved into the neighborhood" (John 1:14 *The Message*).

IN MY OWN JOURNEY WITH JESUS, THERE HAS BEEN NO greater motivation for my faith than the deep, dawning realization that God is one of us. More (far more!) than the hope of heaven or the fear of hell, it is this bedrock belief—that we have seen the face of God in Jesus—that inspires and informs my faith.

The essential reason why is that the person of Jesus has radically altered my meaning for the word God. Let me explain.

For the disciples, those who walked and talked with Jesus, surely there was no greater revelation in their lives than the growing realization that their teacher—whom they would have called Yeshua—was in some mysterious, inexplicable way one with the God they called YHWH.

Again, I don't believe the disciples came to this Jesus-is-God conclusion quickly or lightly, but I am convinced, by the weight of history, that they did come to that astonishing conclusion in time.

But here's the critical point for you and me: the disciples first came to know Jesus as teacher, healer, friend, and king, and then came to know Jesus as God.

Why is that progression so important for us to understand?

Because many of us, if not most, have walked a different path on our journey with Jesus.

We have a somewhat vague meaning in our mind for the word

God—shaped by all sorts of things, ranging from religious traditions to our family backgrounds to a particular reading of Scripture to pop culture. Then, without even realizing it, we bring our view of God to the gospel accounts and unintentionally read the story of Jesus' life through that lens, beginning a long and very often confusing journey of trying to "fit Jesus" into "our meaning" for the word God.[3]

We can find ourselves living in terrible tension at times, with our view of God on one side and our understanding of Jesus on the other, and a chasm of confusion and questions in between.

It's a tension that so many of us can identify with: we've seen and experienced something powerful, compelling, untamed, and true in the person of Jesus, but we have no idea how to reconcile that captivating vision with our sometimes skewed and sometimes even painful views of God.

Good news: you don't have to.

Because the New Testament invites us to do something much more radical than reconcile our skewed views of God with the person of Jesus, something much more fundamental than fitting the story of Jesus' life into our preconceived meaning for the word God.

Instead, the ancient writers seem to say, "Look long and hard at Jesus. Consider his compassion, behold his wisdom, witness his suffering on the cross, experience his resurrection power, and then reshape your vision of God accordingly."

There is no better way to do this than by immersing yourself in the gospel stories of Jesus, which is what I hope to help you do through these pages.

THIS IS A BOOK TO HELP YOU KNOW JESUS, TO IMMERSE YOU in his humanity and brace you with his courage, to refresh you with his humor and baptize you in his tears. My hope is that it will enable you to engage with the gospel stories in a new way, reading them through the gritty lens of Jesus' flesh and blood.

Don't worry, these are not theological treatises. These are down-to-earth gospel readings and reflections exploring what it practically means if God is one of us in Jesus.

The book is divided into five parts:

- Part 1, "Jesus, Mary, and Joseph," focuses on Jesus' family life, with special attention given to the unique relationship he had with his mother.
- Part 2, "Jesus and Abba," looks at the remarkable way Jesus interacted with God—intimate, compelling, and controversial all at once.
- Part 3, "Jesus and His Friends," explores the journey of discipleship that Jesus shared with those who knew him best, his friends and followers.
- Part 4, "Blood, Sweat, and Tears," considers the crucifixion, reflecting on Jesus' trust and determination in the face of confusion, fear, and pain.
- Part 5, "Breakfast on the Beach," is all about the bodily resurrection of Jesus, what it means for us now and for the future.

The readings are brief and meant to be read at your own pace, whether that's multiple chapters in a single sitting or as a forty-day devotional over a few weeks. Each chapter begins with a gospel passage, followed by a reflection, and then wraps up with a final "Ponder, Pray, Practice" section.

The "Ponder, Pray, Practice" sections encourage us to actually do something with what we're learning, and it's difficult to express just how vitally important this part of the Jesus journey is. I'm reminded here of a wise reversal of an old and well-known saying: "While that may work in practice, it will never work in theory."[4]

Following Jesus is a lot like that.

It doesn't work in theory. It works only in practice.

Because faith is not something to be figured out. It's something to be lived.

FINALLY, AS YOU READ, YOU'LL NOTE SOME RECURRING AND significant themes:

- How the person of Jesus radically alters our meaning for the word God.
- How the humanity of Jesus increases our faith to follow him.
- How the unique personality of Jesus, and that of his family and friends, helps us to become more at home in our own skin.

Also, running throughout these pages is an underlying conviction that Jesus' humanity extends a profound and awe-inspiring dignity to our own humanity. Athanasius of Alexandria, an early church father, said it like this: "He became what we are that he might make us what he is."

My primary motive in writing is that Jesus will become more real to you, less of a stained-glass superhero and more of an actual person, and that somewhere along the way, with the help of Holy Spirit, you'll begin to hear the tone of Jesus' voice in the gospel stories and, perhaps, even see the expression on his face.

Because if God is one of us—and that God looks exactly like Jesus— well, that changes everything.

PART ONE

JESUS, MARY, AND JOSEPH

"Isn't he the handyman, Mary's son?"
—MARK 6:3

CHAPTER ONE

ONE HUNDRED DAYS

Jesus came to the town where he had been brought up. He
taught them in their synagogue, and they were astonished.
*   "Where did this fellow get this wisdom, and these*
powers?" they said.
*   "Isn't he the carpenter's son? Isn't his mother called*
Mary, and his brothers James, Joseph, Simon, and Judah?
And aren't all his sisters here with us? So where does he get
it all from?"

—MATTHEW 13:54–56

Practically speaking, we know about Jesus of Nazareth because of two things: his community of followers and the stories they told about him.

Those stories came to us through four ancient documents—the gospels of Matthew, Mark, Luke, and John—and while their accounts agree on most things and disagree on some things, what's most surprising to me is how little of Jesus' life they actually tell.

Think about it. Jesus lived for approximately thirty-three years. That's about twelve thousand days. Of those twelve thousand days, if you add up each and every story the gospel writers tell, those stories account for no more than a hundred days of Jesus' life—total.

One hundred days out of thirty-three years.

That's it. That's what we know. That's all the Bible tells us.

Which just begs the question: What was Jesus doing for most of his life?

ONE OF THE WAYS WE CAN BEGIN TO ANSWER THAT QUES-tion is by considering how Jesus' ministry was accepted in his hometown.

Nazareth was a relatively small place in Jesus' day. About three to four hundred people made up the entire community. Neighbors knew each other in Nazareth. They shared meals with one another. Their sons and daughters played together.

This ancient village, tucked away in a volatile corner of the Roman Empire, is now inextricably linked to the most famous figure in history.

Even though Nazareth's most well-known son would in time be called Christ (or "Anointed King") by hundreds, then thousands, and now millions of people, he is also known by a simpler name, Jesus of Nazareth, a decidedly humble title forever connected to the little community where he grew up.

But, according to gospel accounts, Jesus' hometown had a hard time accepting his ministry. Luke describes it like this:

He came to Nazareth, where he had been brought up. On the sabbath, as was his regular practice, he went into the synagogue and stood up to read. They gave him the scroll of the prophet Isaiah. He unrolled the scroll and found the place where it was written:

The spirit of the Lord is upon me
Because he has anointed me
To tell the poor the good news.
He has sent me to announce release to the prisoners
And sight to the blind,
To set the wounded victims free,
To announce the year of God's special favor.

He rolled up the scroll, gave it to the attendant, and sat down. All eyes in the synagogue were fixed on him.

"Today," he began, "this scripture is fulfilled in your own hearing."

Everyone remarked at him; they were astonished at the words coming out of his mouth—words of sheer grace.

"Isn't this Joseph's son?" they said. (Luke 4:16–22)

One of the reasons Nazareth was "astonished" by what Jesus was saying and doing is because they *knew* him. It's likely that the families of this tightknit Jewish community had known Jesus since he was a little boy.

"Isn't this Joseph's son?" they asked. Or, as the gospel of Matthew puts it, "Isn't he the carpenter's son?" The insinuation, it seems, is that surely Jesus should be following in the footsteps of Joseph, plying his trade as a carpenter in the family business, because apparently, up until now, that's what Jesus had been doing.

THE GOSPEL STORIES WERE GIVEN TO US IN THE GREEK language, and when they refer to Jesus' background in carpentry, the word they use is *tekton*. (Here's what that word looks like in Greek: τέκτων.)

Now, *tekton* does not necessarily mean carpenter, as in a person who makes and repairs exclusively wooden things. Instead, *tekton* means something more general, like craftsman, as in a person who works with their hands.*

Because the gospel writers make no specific reference to wood or stone, we can assume that Jesus may well have been capable working with both of these materials, and perhaps with metal too. The point is

---

* Our English word architect comes from the Greek word *arkhitekton*, which basically means "master builder." Here's how it works: *arkhi-* ("chief") + *tekton* ("craftsman") = chief craftsman.

not whether Jesus was a woodworker, a stonemason, or a blacksmith. The point is that Jesus was a workman. He had a trade.

While Jesus was growing up, there was a significant building project just north of Nazareth in a bustling city called Sepphoris. One can't help but wonder if young Jesus worked for a time in Sepphoris, about a twenty-minute walk from his hometown, as an apprentice craftsman alongside Joseph and other builders from Nazareth:

> Imagine him there, carefully measuring each cut of the cedar, sweat dripping from his brow, his back, the creases of his elbows, sawdust clinging to his clothes: Can you see him?

Trained as a *tekton* and surrounded by other day laborers: Is this why Jesus later seemed so at home with blue-collar workmen in his inner circle? Is this why his down-to-earth and deeply insightful parables include imagery of storage barns and watchtowers, millstones and splinters, earthy objects so familiar to the life and trade of a builder?

Is this one of the reasons why the Nazarene was such a magnetic figure in the first century, a true "man of the people," in the best sense of the phrase, because he really was one of them?

SO TO ANSWER OUR QUESTION: WHAT WAS JESUS DOING FOR most of his life?

Jesus was doing what each and every one of us does. He was working and resting, learning and growing, eating and thinking, laughing and mourning, and day by day discerning his vocation, and Jesus was doing all of that with friends and family in the enjoyable and challenging context of the community he called home.

Here's the vital point for you and me: all of life was important to Jesus because all of life is important to God.

Jesus was no more holy as a rabbi (teacher) than he was as a *tekton*, was he? Of course he wasn't. In the same way, regardless of what you do today—whether that's writing a paper, planting a garden, preparing a work proposal, or parenting a child—what you're doing is important to God because it's part of being human.

And Jesus understands exactly what that means.

Ponder. What part of being human is it most difficult for you to imagine Jesus participating in with you? Why is that?

Pray. Give thanks for your "everyday, ordinary life,"* and then ask God to open your eyes to the overlooked wonders and underappreciated people all around you.

Practice. Visualize each and every part of your day (your relationships, your mealtimes, your work, your play, etc.), and invite God into all of it.

---

* The phrase "everyday, ordinary life" comes from Romans 12:1 in *The Message*, and the complete passage reads like this: "So here's what I want you to do, God helping you: Take your everyday, ordinary life—your sleeping, eating, going-to-work, and walking-around life—and place it before God as an offering."

CHAPTER TWO

"OH, MOTHER!"

On the third day there was a wedding at Cana in Galilee.
Jesus' mother was there, and Jesus and his disciples were
also invited to the wedding.
> *The wine ran out.*
> *Jesus's mother came over to him.*
> *"They haven't got any wine!" she said.*
> *"Oh, Mother!" replied Jesus. "What's that got to do with*
you and me? My time hasn't come yet."
> *His mother spoke to the servants. "Do whatever he tells*
you," she said.
> —JOHN 2:1–5

Nonverbal communication accounts for most of what we say—our tone of voice, facial expressions, the look in our eyes, even our posture—and one of the real challenges in reading the gospel accounts is that they rarely include these sorts of nonverbal clues.

Consider that perplexing wedding scene at Cana, where Jesus and his mother share what appears to be a testy interchange. Jesus seems to resist, even bristle at his mom's insistence that he help remedy an embarrassing situation for the bride and groom.

"Oh, Mother!" Jesus says. "What's that got to do with you and me? My time hasn't come yet." (You can almost hear the borderline exasperation in Jesus' voice, can't you?)

But Mother Mary, for reasons unseen, understands this curious response from her firstborn differently. Instead of hearing no, she hears yes. Instead of being hurt by her son's blunt response, Mary is somehow now assured that Jesus will intervene.

"Do whatever he tells you," she instructs the waiting servants.

So what made the difference? What did Mary experience in this unusual interchange with her son that so many of us miss?

IF A PICTURE IS WORTH A THOUSAND WORDS, THEN THERE must be inestimable value in imagining—picturing in our minds—the vivid and telling expressions that crossed Jesus' face every day (and still do).

Before we explore this ancient wedding scene a little further, though, let's first continue with John's narrative:

Six stone water-jars were standing there, ready for use in the Jewish purification rites. Each held about twenty or thirty gallons.

"Fill the jars with water," said Jesus to the servants. And they filled them, right up to the brim.

"Now draw some out," he said, "and take it to the chief steward." They did so.

When the chief steward tasted the water that had turned into wine (he didn't know where it had come from, but the servants who had drawn the water knew), he called the bridegroom.

"What everybody normally does," he said, "is to serve the good wine first, and then the worse stuff when people have had plenty to drink. But you've kept the good wine till now!"

This event, in Cana of Galilee, was the first of Jesus' signs. He displayed his glory, and his disciples believed in him. (John 2:6–11)

Now, other than that confusing conversation with his mom at the start (and don't worry, we'll get back to that critical point), it's hard not to like Jesus in this story, isn't it?

Think about it: the most famous figure in history doesn't launch his public career by healing someone, casting out demons, or delivering an inspiring speech—yes, those things take place in time too—but here, at the celebration in Cana, the "first of Jesus' signs" is turning water into wine to keep a party going strong, rescuing a bridegroom and his bride from certain shame on their wedding day.

A Jewish wedding in the first century was a village affair, with celebrations lasting up to a full week. It was the honor and responsibility of the bridegroom and his family to host. When the wine runs out and Jesus decides to intervene, he does so quietly. He doesn't take the honor away from the bridegroom:

> When the chief steward tasted the water that had turned into wine (he didn't know where it had come from, but the servants who had drawn the water knew), he called the bridegroom.
>
> "What everybody normally does," he said, "is to serve the good wine first, and then the worse stuff when people have had plenty to drink. But you've kept the good wine till now!"

Isn't that just like Jesus? Saving the day by turning water into wine, honoring the bewildered bridegroom before the chief steward and all the guests, and letting only "the servants" and his disciples in on the secret.

BUT WHAT ABOUT MOTHER MARY AND THAT ABRUPT BEGINning? If the narrative lands on such a high note—with the party saved, the servants stunned, and the disciples believing—then why the negative note at the start?

The only way I can understand that important part of the story is by recognizing that something nonverbal took place between Jesus and his mom in that moment. There must have been something in the look of his eyes, in the tone of his voice, in the expression on his face that communicated more than words could say to Mary.

This moment in Cana marks a significant turning point in Jesus' journey, which is most likely why it is referred to in John as "the first of his signs." From here forward, Jesus is steadily moving toward his destined vocation as Messiah.

Remember, while the disciples (and probably his mom too) understood the role of Messiah to mean something like Conquering King (the one who would defeat Rome), Jesus understood the role of Messiah to mean something more like Crucified King (the one who will be killed by Rome).

Jesus knows, in the deepest part of him, that once this journey begins and his identity as Messiah is revealed, it will ultimately lead to his suffering and death. Because that's what being King looks like for Jesus: the journey begins at a party, but it leads to the blood, sweat, and tears of the cross.

No wonder he's a little abrupt with his mom.

Amazingly, even as his initial response flashes with the agony that awaits him, something in Jesus' face seems to soften at the same time, and his mother, this brave woman who has known him since birth, sees it.

While we cannot know for sure what passed between Jesus and Mary in that poignant moment, with a wedding party and the weight of the world hanging in the balance, I think it is safe to say that something in the look of Jesus' eyes clearly communicated, "Don't worry, Mom. I'll take care of it—all of it."

"Do whatever he tells you," Mary says to the waiting servants.

Water is transformed into wine, a wedding party in Cana is saved, and King Jesus begins his three-year journey to the cross, all of it turning on a silent exchange between a son and his mother.

Ponder. If Jesus is alive, there is a look on his face right now. What do you think it is?

Pray. Ask Holy Spirit to help you reimagine the stories of Jesus—that you would learn to recognize the look in his eyes, the expression on his face, even the tone of his voice.

Practice. With this new way of reading in mind, quiet your soul for three minutes and reread the story of the wedding feast in Cana in John 2:1–10.

CHAPTER THREE

DEFENDING MARY

"Isn't he the handyman, Mary's son?"
—MARK 6:3

Mark was the first of the four gospel accounts to be written, and it's quite a big deal that the author includes a description of Jesus as Mary's son.

In the ancient world, you rarely (if ever) described a person in a historical record by the name of their mother. It was almost always by the name of their father. When you come to a similar account in the gospel of Matthew, for example, Jesus is called "the carpenter's son." In the gospel of Luke, he is "Joseph's son."

But here, in this standout moment in Mark, Jesus is called "Mary's son." Why?

This unusual description in the earliest gospel reflects a controversial issue that dogged Jesus for most of his life. To put it bluntly, people had legitimate questions about what they perceived to be Jesus' illegitimate background.

Because of the unusual circumstances surrounding his birth, Jesus may well have been known as a *mamzer* (pronounced *mom-zer*) his entire life. *Mamzer* is a Hebrew word, and its use in reference to Jesus means there were serious questions about who Jesus' father was.

"All languages have a word for *mamzer*," explains pastor John Ortberg in *Who Is This Man?* "and all of them are ugly."[5]

There's a telling story in the gospel of John when some religious leaders openly confront Jesus over this point. In three different translations of John 8:41, here is how the most intense moment of that confrontation reads:

- "There wasn't anything immoral about the way *we* were born!"
- "We aren't illegitimate children!" (NLT).
- "We're not bastards" (*The Message*).

Regardless of how you read it, the accusation is the same, and, as you might expect, that sort of talk sets Jesus off. According to John, Jesus fiercely responds to the leaders, "You are from your father—the devil!" (8:44).

Let's be clear about what is happening here: That is a son defending the honor of his mother. Jesus is striking back at the suggestion that Mary had in some way been immoral. Because, as we all know, you don't talk about someone's mother.

WHEN I WAS NINE YEARS OLD MY BEST FRIEND BEAT UP THE school bully. At the time, it was one of the greatest days of my life.

The school bully that year was a kid named Calvin. Whenever our teacher left the classroom, Calvin selected some innocent soul to make suffer. If you've ever been bullied—because of your size, your looks, your family—then you know the panicked feeling that rushes your chest when a teacher steps out of the classroom and a bully takes over.

It was that sort of feeling I was experiencing one day when our teacher disappeared through the classroom door to speak with someone in the hallway. While I had managed to avoid Calvin's ire that year so far, I knew my time was coming, and I sensed it was here at last.

For whatever reason, though, Calvin directed his gaze that day toward my best friend, Steven Shinn, instead.

Steven was one of the biggest kids in class, but he never hurt or bothered anyone. He was a tall, sometimes hefty, sometimes lanky kid who drank more milk than anyone I knew. In my eyes, my best friend,

Steven, was a gentle giant, the kind of kid who rarely got upset, but when he did, he would cry.

When Calvin taunted Steven that day, calling him all sorts of names, I knew it was affecting him, because Steven's eyes were filling with tears. I wanted to intervene, to somehow make it stop, but I was afraid. We all were.

The problem with a bully is that tears can embolden them. Once Calvin realized the effect he was having, he decided to push even further by saying something about Steven's mom.

I'll never forget what happened next.

Steven closed his eyes for a moment and the tears brimmed over. Without saying a word, he took Calvin by his shirt collar with one hand and by the inside of his thigh with the other. Steven lifted Calvin off his feet, held him briefly above the ground, and then—in a raw and wildly inspiring feat of nine-year-old adrenaline—my best friend, Steven Shinn, threw the school bully into a desk.

At that moment, as if on cue, a roomful of nine-year-old kids went ballistic. In our little world, dominated by fear for far too long, the tide had turned at last, the school bully had been defeated, and we were *free*—yes, finally, free.

I still remember that amazing moment as if it were yesterday. Kids were cheering, tears were streaming, and I was in the back of the classroom yelling, "Yes! Yes! Yes!" Because I had never been so proud of my best friend.

Calvin never bullied Steven again. (For the record, he never bullied me either, because I was Steven's best friend—see how that works?) The school bully had learned an important lesson: you don't talk about someone's mother.

JESUS DIDN'T DECK THE RELIGIOUS LEADERS WHO DISHON-ored his mom, but the important question for you and me is this: Did he want to?

When you witness raw moments of emotion like this in the gospel, with Jesus fiercely defending the honor of his mother and going so far as to say these leaders were fathered by the devil, you understand that Jesus was a man of great passion.

He didn't float through the first century as an emotionless, ghostlike figure exercising some sort of divine, escapist exemption from real feelings. On the contrary, Jesus was known for his tears (like my friend Steven) and for his frustrations, he was known for his witty sayings and his sometimes-cutting convictions.

Why have we sought to transform Jesus into someone else, into this stoic, emotion-free figure we so often assume him to be?

I was recently discussing this question with a close friend, and shortly after our conversation he related to me (via email) the following story about his father:

> When my dad was a young boy, maybe six or eight years old, his parents made him attend Sunday school. He remembers his teacher telling him "Jesus was *perfect*, and Jesus *never* sinned. He never did a bad thing or had a single bad thought. So we should all try to be like him."
>
> My dad said that presentation pretty much made him give up on the idea of Jesus right off the bat . . . He could not identify with this person—or really even with the *idea* of this person.

One of the reasons why good-hearted Sunday school teachers, professionally trained ministers, and plenty of other people, too, unintentionally mute Jesus' emotions is because we are afraid of what those emotions might mean.

"If Jesus actually wanted to punch the leaders who were talking about his mom," we reason, "wouldn't that mean he was somehow subject to the power of sin?"

No, it would just mean he was in no way immune to the power of emotion! It would mean, actually, that Jesus felt things deeply, like we all do, but that, thankfully, he was not controlled, consumed, or mastered by those feelings.

Now, as to what Jesus would say to my friend Steven about how he handled that situation when we were nine, I can't say for sure. But I can tell you this: Jesus didn't like it when someone talked smack about his mom.

Ponder. Given his curious birth, what do you think it was like for Jesus growing up?

Pray. Ask Holy Spirit to help you know how to respond when you are bullied by someone in power, when you are unjustly accused or deeply misunderstood.

Practice. In some simple way, like sharing a meal with someone who needs a friend or by reaching out to someone who may feel alone, spend time with the vulnerable today.

CHAPTER FOUR

JOSEPH AND JESUS

This was how the birth of Jesus the Messiah took place.
His mother, Mary, was engaged to Joseph; but before
they came together she turned out to be pregnant—by the
holy spirit.
Joseph, her husband-to-be, was an upright man. He
didn't want to make a public example of her. So he decided
to set the marriage aside privately.
—MATTHEW 1:18–19

Joseph is considered a saint by most Christian traditions, and for good reason too, but Mary might have begged to differ with that saintly assessment on the day Joseph did not believe her.

Consider the chain of events:

- Joseph and Mary are engaged.
- Mary turns out to be pregnant.
- Joseph is not the father.
- Mary claims she is innocent.
- Joseph does not believe her.

How do we know that Joseph did not believe Mary? The narrative is quite clear: "he decided to set the marriage aside."

Joseph does not want to publicly shame his tarnished bride-to-be, so he determines to take care of the delicate and embarrassing task of breaking their engagement privately instead of insisting on a public trial. Their betrothal, it should be understood, was already legally binding in its first-century setting.

Regardless of how the separation would happen, whether privately or publicly, it is clear that Joseph will do what must be done. While Mary has made her decision and she must now live with the consequences, Joseph's reputation is still intact.

> But, while he was considering this, an angel of the Lord suddenly appeared to him in a dream.
>
> "Joseph, son of David," the angel said, "Don't be afraid to get married to Mary. The child she is carrying is from the holy spirit." (Matt. 1:20)

Imagine Joseph waking up from that dream, the realization dawning that when Mary needed him the most, he had believed the worst.

MUCH HAS BEEN MADE OF JESUS' GROUNDBREAKING INTER-action with women, and I can't help but wonder if Joseph was not a formative and perhaps even decisive influence shaping Jesus' exceptional views in this area.*

Joseph had misjudged Mary—he had believed the worst about her—and that regrettable moment of misjudgment must have marked Joseph deeply.

Yes, there are plenty of honest and understandable reasons why he misjudged her, not least that Mary was pregnant and Joseph knew

---

* Whether it's the woman at the well in the gospel of John (4:4–30), the female disciple in the gospel of Luke (10:38–42), or the fascinating historical anomaly that all four gospel accounts record women as the first witnesses of Jesus' resurrection (a point we'll explore in part 5), the way Jesus related to women is striking in its first-century setting.

he was not the father. But if we believe this story is true (and I do), Mary deserved Joseph's trust, regardless of what the circumstances looked like.

Instead, Joseph became the first in a long line of men and women alike who have simply not believed Mary was telling the truth.

Maybe this is a small part of what that old man Simeon meant when he met Mary and Joseph in the Temple while they were dedicating their firstborn son to God, took the infant Jesus in his arms, and said to his young mother:

> "This child has been placed here to make many in Israel fall and rise again, and as a sign that will be spoken against *(yes, a sword will go through your own soul as well)*, so that the thoughts of many hearts may be disclosed." (Luke 2:34, italics added)

Think about it: Has there ever been a woman in the history of the world whose sexual reputation has been analysed, discussed, and debated more than Mary's? In so many ways, surely a sword has pierced her soul.

When Joseph asked Mary to forgive him for not trusting her, he was not only confessing his wrong, he was embracing her shame. The questions that swirled around Mary's unplanned pregnancy would now swirl around Joseph too.

Remember, a Jewish wedding in the first century was a villagewide event, with celebrations lasting up to a full week as festivities moved from house to house. That would not be the case, though, if a couple was expecting a child out of wedlock, a couple like Mary and Joseph.

Instead of celebrations, there would be questions. In place of festivities, there would be hushed conversations. And the woman, as is so often the case in this sort of circumstance, would carry the greater shame.

But Mary would not bear this burden alone, because Joseph was there.

THE GOSPEL OF JOHN TELLS THE STORY OF A WOMAN "caught in the act of adultery" who has been brought to Jesus for judgment.

Her male partner has either fled the scene or has been let go by the authorities, and the woman is now facing a brutalizing trial of public opinion—alone. After outlining the charges against the woman, her accusers put Jesus to the test:

> "Teacher," they said to him. "This woman was caught in the very act of adultery. In the law, Moses commanded us to stone people like this. What do you say?"
>
> They said this to test him, so that they could frame a charge against him.
>
> Jesus squatted down and wrote with his finger on the ground.
>
> When they went on pressing the question, he got up and said to them, "Whichever of you is without sin should throw the first stone at her."

The story eventually wraps up with the men walking away, one by one, leaving the woman alone with Jesus, who refuses to condemn her (John 8:3–11).

Was Jesus aware in that moment his mother might easily have found herself in a similar situation, surrounded by glaring accusers on every side with no one to defend her, had it not been for Joseph?

How many times, I wonder, did Jesus watch Joseph protect Mary's reputation, always at the cost of his own? Something happens in a boy when he sees his dad defend his mother, and when it comes to influential father figures in this regard, Joseph undoubtedly ranks very high.

We don't know exactly how or when Joseph died, but according to tradition, Joseph died in the arms of Mary and Jesus before Jesus started his public ministry. The specifics may vary, but most biblical scholars agree with that assessment because Joseph's absence is so glaring in the gospel accounts after Jesus becomes an adult.

Joseph would not be there to see his son heal the blind or preach to the masses. He would not witness his boy bravely confronting the establishment and paying such an awful price for it.

But as Joseph lay dying, cared for by his longsuffering and courageous wife, I imagine he could let go of this life confident that Mary would be okay, because he knew that his son Jesus would always be there to defend her.

Ponder. Fathers have tremendous influence in the lives of their children, and Jesus must have felt the loss of Joseph deeply. Jesus likely knows what it means to have a single parent.

Pray. Ask Holy Spirit to help you learn from, forgive, and honor your parents.

Practice. Think of one significant way in which your parents or parentlike figures in your life have shaped you for the better—and, if they're still living, tell them.

CHAPTER FIVE

BLUNTLY PUT

After eight days, the time came to circumcise the baby.
—LUKE 2:21

When I was a kid, one of my favorite Christmas carols was "Away in a Manger," particularly that part in the second verse that says, "The cattle are lowing, the poor baby awakes; But little Lord Jesus, no crying he makes."

I would sing that part with all my heart, imagining Jesus on the night of his birth, his "little Lord" eyes peering into distant galaxies, with not a tear in sight. That was before I had children of my own, though, and it was before I understood what the word circumcise means.

Like most Jewish boys in the first century, Jesus was circumcised on the eighth day of his life. Circumcision was a sign of God's covenant with the Hebrew people. This ancient practice was initiated with Father Abraham, codified by Moses, and then passed down to each generation of Jewish males.*

---

* A fascinating theory as to why both Genesis and Leviticus instruct that boys should be circumcised on the eighth day has to do with how blood clotting works in a newborn baby. The human body has two blood-clotting factors: vitamin K and prothrombin. Vitamin K is not formed in our bodies until five to seven days after we are born, and prothrombin peaks in our bodies on the eighth day.

Scientists did not discover these two blood-clotting phenomena until the 1930s, and soon after began recommending vitamin K injections for all newborn babies to prevent the development of serious bleeding disorders. Thousands of years before, however, a nomadic Hebrew tribe was already waiting until the eighth day to circumcise their infant sons, the perfect time to prevent hemorrhaging in a newborn child.

Male circumcision is a painful procedure to watch, even more so to endure. The foreskin of the penis, one of the most vulnerable and intimate areas of the male anatomy, is swiftly removed with one careful slice of a blade.

There is lots of debate as to whether there are enough significant health benefits for baby boys to still be circumcised, and regardless of where you stand on that issue, it's important for us to recognize that a great deal of that debate centers on the subject of pain. Bluntly put: circumcision hurts.

While the gospel writers feel no need to address whether little Lord Jesus cried at his birth, I think we can be confident that he shed some real tears on the eighth day of his life.

I WAS AN UNCLE BEFORE I WAS A FATHER, AND I THINK IT works well that way. It's a bit like being baptized by water and then by fire—the water surprises you, the flames refine you.

It's not that my nephews and nieces didn't at times present their uncle with some pretty serious predicaments to deal with (including one nephew defecating on my arm the first day of his life). It's just that all of their issues (especially their bodily functions and the unending care they require) were not my responsibility.

I could help their parents clean up after them, but I certainly didn't have to.

Parenting my own children, on the other hand, presented me with a new set of rules. Now, each and every time something comes out of one of the small humans who live with us (and it happens with alarming frequency), it is my responsibility to do something about it.

Let me give you a few examples.

My oldest daughter once vomited on a plane, all over herself and all over the seat, just as the aircraft was touching down.

What was I to do with all of that?

My son, while lying peacefully on a changing table, once urinated in a perfectly formed arch onto his own forehead.

How are you supposed to care for a crying child when you're laughing so hard it hurts?

My youngest daughter produced such an impressive amount of meconium (the technical term for an infant's first bowel movement) that I had to yell for help.

What do you do when you run out of wipes but your newborn hasn't run out of poo?

Do we honestly think Mary and Joseph didn't have similar stories to tell about baby Jesus?

We imagine him as an unusually bright little boy, and surely he was, but that doesn't mean Jesus was somehow supernaturally potty-trained as a toddler.

We read and sing about the Christ child wrapped in swaddling clothes, but we must keep in mind the fabric was smeared with blood and vernix and amniotic fluid from his birth.

We picture him the perfect infant, resting peacefully in Mary's arms, but if the "cattle are lowing" and "the poor baby awakes," I doubt that "no crying he makes."

GNOSTICISM IS A FUNNY-SOUNDING WORD WITH SERIOUS implications. Basically, it describes a collection of ancient worldviews and writings that looked down on physical reality and exalted the spiritual world in its place.

Unfortunately, many of us view Jesus through this sort of lens. I think this is one of the primary reasons we have such a hard time relating to him.

Often there is a great divide in our minds between the physical and the spiritual. (For what it's worth, this way of thinking has little to do with the influence of Jesus and a whole lot to do with the influence of

Plato.) We categorize things into sacred or secular, natural or super-natural. The person of Jesus, we reason, most naturally fits into the spiritual/sacred/supernatural side of things.

For the first-century Jewish mind, however—and we must always remember that Jesus and his earliest followers were all first-century Jews—the great divide between the physical and the spiritual did not necessarily exist.

We witness this undivided reality in their most sacred/spiritual of records, the Torah, where practical/physical instruction is provided about the most earthy of activities: about how to handle the bloody cloths from a woman's period (Lev. 15:20), about where to bury one's excrement after a bowel movement (Deut. 23:13), and yes, about which day is best for a baby boy to be circumcised (Lev. 12:3).

The reason I bring up these down-to-earth Torah examples is because they are human experiences, the sort of things Jesus experienced. And it's vitally important to keep that in mind, lest we fall prey to that old gnostic temptation of splitting everything up into physical versus spiritual.

Two thousand years of history, theology, and poetry have at times blinded us to the vulnerable beauty of a newborn baby who cooed, cried, and "went potty" just like the rest of us.

Don't get me wrong, I still love to sing "Away in a Manger" at Christmastime—really, I do—I just sing the old hymn a little differently now: "The cattle are lowing, the poor baby awakes; And little Lord Jesus, *some* crying he makes."[6]

Ponder. Mary and Joseph were probably in awe at the circumstances surrounding Jesus' birth, but during those first few days of his life, they may well have had more pressing matters on their minds, like what to do with the meconium.

Pray. Ask that you won't fall prey to that old gnostic temptation of dividing everything up into physical versus spiritual, resulting in a low view of the body and a weird view of Jesus.

Practice. Sometimes, the best thing for your spirit is to do something with your body, like taking a brief walk outside when you're feeling heavy in heart.

CHAPTER SIX

EVERYMAN

"You are to give him the name Jesus; he is the one who will save his people from their sins."
—MATTHEW 1:21

When I'm waiting for a table at a restaurant, I occasionally give the server a false name. Nine times out of ten, that name is Carl. The only explanation I can provide for this unusual behavior is that some friends of mine in the UK, where I lived and worked for eight years, used to regularly refer to me as Carl Swifty.

While the Carl part of my nickname is inexplicable, the Swifty part comes from the fact that *Trent* really does mean "swift." (And yes, in case you're wondering, I am unusually fast.)

Typically, names tell us a thing or two about the person they are describing. Clark Kent, for instance, is a mild-mannered reporter for the *Daily Planet*. His alter ego, Superman, on the other hand, possesses unearthly powers, hails from the planet Krypton, and "is faster than a speeding bullet."

Diana Prince is the unassuming alias of Wonder Woman, the Amazonian superheroine who lives and works in a world dominated by men. At times she's a secretary, at others a nurse, but as soon as Diana Prince starts spinning (which is how she becomes Wonder Woman), you had best take cover.

Bruce Wayne is a brash billionaire and philanthropist in Gotham

City. What the people of Gotham don't realize is that Bruce Wayne is also Batman, a mysterious crime-fighting warlord, skilled in the martial arts, with a vast cache of ingenious tools that somehow seem to always keep him one step ahead of the bad guys.

Superman. Batman. Wonder Woman. (Carl Swifty?) Each of these characters is a superhero, and it's their names that tell us why.

The name Jesus, however, tells a different story.

ACCORDING TO FIRST-CENTURY JEWISH HISTORIAN JOSE-phus, the name Jesus was one of the most common names of its time, a bit like being called John Smith today.

Jesus wasn't a name that stood out from the rest. On the contrary, when Mary or Joseph reminded their son to stay close in a crowded marketplace—calling aloud for him, "Jesus!"—a number of little boys probably would have turned their heads in response.

Describing just how common the name Jesus was in its ancient Near East setting, Catholic professor and Pulitzer Prize–winning author Gary Wills says it like this in his little book *What Jesus Meant*: "It is as if he were called Everyman."[7]

Everyman.

Not Superman.

Everyman.

I think this Everyman identity is what the author of Hebrews is getting at when he (or is it she?)* compares Jesus to a high priest in the Temple: "We don't have a priest who is out of touch with our reality.

---

* The identity of the writer behind the letter to the Hebrews has long been a mystery. While Barnabas, Apollos, and even the gospel writer Luke are all a possibility, some historians suggest it may well have been Priscilla, who alongside her husband, Aquila, is described by the apostle Paul as one of "my fellow workers in King Jesus" (Rom. 16:3). Supporting this view is the fact that Hebrews is one of the only epistles in the New Testament whose author intentionally remains anonymous, which has led some scholars to wonder if Priscilla chose to keep her authorship a secret because she was living (and leading) in a world dominated by men.

He's been through weakness and testing, experienced it all—all but the sin" (4:15 *The Message*).

Earlier in Hebrews, a similar point is made:

That's why [Jesus] had to be like his brothers and sisters *in every way*, so that he might become a merciful and trustworthy high priest in God's presence, to make atonement for the sins of the people. He himself has suffered, you see, through being put to the test, and that's why he is able to help those who are being tested right now. (2:17–18, italics added)

But what do those words mean—that Jesus experienced it all, that he was like the rest of us in every way?

Well, among other things, I think they mean that Jesus knows what it's like for a five-year-old to feel left out, because he's been there.

I think it means he understands how challenging it can be for a thirteen-year-old kid to hit puberty, because he's experienced it.

I think it means we have a "high priest" who doesn't abandon us when we doubt the core tenets of our faith, the religious traditions in which we've been raised, and even the purpose and power of prayer, because Jesus, we must understand, wrestled in prayer too.

That's the thing about Jesus: he gets it, he really does. Because he's not some sort of a stained-glass superhero. He's Everyman.

JESUS IS THE GREEK AND ENGLISH TRANSLITERATION OF the Hebrew name Yeshua. That's what his friends and family called him, Yeshua. (I can't help but wonder if they ever called him Yeshu for short, or perhaps even just Yesh.)

When I imagine Jesus in his first-century setting, especially when I picture him as a child, I think it helps to keep in mind that his name was pronounced differently than we say it now. He's not that sandy-blond, blue-eyed Scandinavian guy-god with a Greek-English name we've made him out to be.

Rather, he's a tousled-haired, brown-eyed little Jewish boy with lots of dust on his clothes and a precocious look on his face—yes, that's young Yeshua.

And when we see Jesus in this light—in the light of Yeshua—it tells us something astounding about what we mean by the word God. In the ancient Hebrew writings, God was revealed in multiple ways:

- "In the beginning . . ." as maker of light, matter, and humanity (Genesis 1).
- To Moses, as the fiery and invincible YHWH, the great "I Am" (Exodus 3).
- To the people, a pillar of cloud by day, a pillar of light by night (Exodus 13).

But the writer of Hebrews suggests that something much more radical, something much more fundamental is at work in the person of Jesus:

> In many ways and by many means, God spoke in ancient days to our ancestors in the prophets; but at the end of these days he spoke to us in a son . . . the shining reflection of God's own glory, the *precise expression* of his own very being. (Heb. 1:1–3, italics added)

Consider the sheer weight of those words: "the precise expression" of God. It's a wildly audacious claim, to say the least. For what we could not know in majesty (maybe because it was just too much for us to handle) has at last been revealed to us in childlike humility.

It turns out the glory of God has a face: Jesus (2 Cor. 4:6).

This way of seeing God—finally, and most accurately, through the person of Jesus—reshapes our theology in the deepest and most meaningful of ways:

Because it means God is close: close enough to be touched in Jesus.

Because it means God, while remaining all-powerful, is somehow vulnerable: vulnerable enough to bleed and die in Jesus.

And, perhaps most moving (especially when it comes to our hurting humanity and the confusion, fear, and yearning that so often come with it), because it means that God, the maker of heaven and earth, really does understand what it means to be human.

Ponder. We will never see God more clearly or more truly than in the person of Jesus.

Pray. Give God your fears, your sin, your confusion, even your pain, because Jesus understands what it means to be human—really, he does.

Practice. Begin repenting of your un-Jesus-like views of God. (Repenting simply means changing your mind and, as a result, changing your actions.)

CHAPTER SEVEN

WISER AND TALLER

Jesus became wiser and taller, gaining favor both with God and with the people.

—LUKE 2:52

Before our children go to bed, I pray a simple prayer with them that they will grow "in wisdom, in stature, and in favor with God and people," just like Jesus grew.

"Daddy," I'm occasionally asked during those prayers, "what's wisdom?"

"Well, wisdom is learning how to make good choices.

"It basically just means that when you've got a big decision to make, you'll know what to do. Like deciding whether to share something that's very special to you," I explain. "Or, when you're older, like deciding whom you will marry."

"Like how you married Mommy?" my eldest daughter asks.

"Exactly," I smile.

I kiss our kids, tell them it's time to sleep, and quietly close their bedroom door. Just outside, standing in the hallway, I wait awhile to make sure they're settled.

Waiting and listening, I begin to wonder:

If Jesus and God are one, how on earth did Jesus grow in wisdom? I mean, didn't Jesus just know what to do, and do the right thing, simply because he was Jesus?

"Whew," I whisper out loud, "I sure am glad the kids didn't ask me that."

Just then, a little voice on the other side of the door interrupts the quiet.

"Daddy, are you still there? I've got one more question."

WHEN IT COMES TO THE INCARNATION, THE EARLY CHRIS-tian conviction that Jesus of Nazareth was and is God in flesh and blood and bones, it's important to understand we are dealing with a mystery shrouded in overwhelming wonder.

I'm at peace with that mystery, at peace that God is God and I am not. There are a great many things in life we don't completely understand. If God is not one of them, then perhaps, in the classic words of J. B. Phillips, "Your God is too small."

At the same time, though, just because we cannot fully understand the incarnation does not mean that we should not explore the incarnation in as much depth as we can.

T. F. Torrance (1913–2007) was a Scottish professor and preacher world renowned for his pioneering and integrative work in theology and science, and he was also keenly interested in searching out the profound and practical reality of what the incarnation means.

In a collection of his published lectures, TFT (that's what his students called him) explores the fascinating passage in Luke that speaks of Jesus' growing in wisdom. "From the very start," explains Torrance, "Luke tells us, in an astonishing word about the growth of Jesus, *proekopten*, that he had to beat his way forward by blows. His obedience was a battle."[8]

So what is TFT getting at when he suggests that "obedience was a battle" for Jesus, that he "had to beat his way forward by blows"?

It all centers on the word *proekopten* (which, by the way, looks like this in Greek: προέκοπτεν). Luke chooses a word that basically means "to beat" to explain how Jesus grew or increased in wisdom.

Proekopten portrays something akin to the machete-like action of a pioneer: beating/cutting/carving a pathway through dense, overgrown wilderness. It can also lend itself to the imagery of an ironsmith: pounding/molding/beating a piece of red-hot metal against a rock-solid anvil.[9]

Luke's point in using this "astonishing" word to describe Jesus' character growth is partly that he wants us to understand that Jesus grew in wisdom just like the rest of us do—by making hard choices to do what is good, right, and true, even when we feel the temptation to do something else.

BEING HUMAN IS NOT ALWAYS EASY, IS IT? WHEN I WAS FOURteen years old, in that vulnerable, awkward, and truly perplexing period of life known as puberty, I learned I had a skin disease called psoriasis.

Plenty of people have psoriasis. It looks a bit like eczema, and it can make various parts of your body very scaly, very itchy, and very uncomfortable.

For lots of people, psoriasis can be managed with certain creams, ointments, and shampoos and by paying careful attention to their overall health. In rare cases, it can affect large portions of the body, require ongoing medical care, and, as a result, lead to pretty serious depression.

I was one of the rare cases, and, seriously, it couldn't have hit at a worse time. Because when puberty and psoriasis crossed paths in my body and mind, I was faced with the very worst version of me.

I was fiercely angry, punching walls as hard as I could at times. I was raging with hormones, you know, typical early teenage puberty. Worst of all, I was stubborn and proud, and I pushed people away, convinced that no one—*no one!*—could possibly understand what I was going through.

As a result, I became deeply sad, because I didn't know what to do with all the rage in my heart, all the lust in my mind, and all the scabs on my body.

What followed were several painful years of internal wrestling and a lot of ups and downs. My body, mind, and heart began to heal, but not without some big changes.

With psoriasis, it primarily came through health changes and the care of doctors.

With my thought life, it was through confession, prayer, and real accountability.

With anger, it was by a searing revelation that I didn't want to be a rage-full man.*

Some twenty-five years have now passed, and I must confess: character growth in each of these areas has never come easily for me. Because making the hard choice to do what is good, right, and true is a battle—it still is—but it's a battle worth fighting.

LIFE WASN'T EFFORTLESS FOR JESUS, WITH ALL THE CHAL-lenging decisions made for him. No, according to Luke, Jesus had "to beat" his way forward—moment by moment, choice by choice, day after day, year after year—as he *became* wiser.

We don't know the circumstances, temptations, and challenges Jesus faced during his hidden years, but we do know that those circumstances, temptations, and challenges did not define, control, or overcome him.

Jesus never gave in to unrighteous rage.

He never gave in to the controlling power of lust.

He never gave in to thinking more highly of himself than others.

He never gave in to [insert your ongoing battle].

Again, keep in mind how Jesus is described in the book of Hebrews, as "tempted in every way just as we are, yet without sin." Amazingly, the writer doesn't stop there: "Let us then come boldly to the throne

---

* My older brother was like a live-in priest to me during this time, hearing my confessions and helping me pray. And it was in this same season of life that my older sister shared with me a simple and life-transforming thought about Jesus and anger that changed my understanding: "Jesus got angry too," she told me, "but he only lost his cool over areas of evil and injustice."

of grace," the verse continues, "so that we may receive mercy, and may find grace to help us at the moment when we need it" (4:15–16).

The critical point is this: we can come to Jesus with our messy, broken, sinful lives because Jesus knows how hard it is to be human, because he knows obedience is a battle.

Ponder. What consistently challenging choice must you make, and what changes do you need to implement to become wiser in that area?

Pray. Ask Holy Spirit to help you grow in wisdom, just like Jesus. (Don't feel like you have to have everything figured out all at once. If Jesus had time to grow, we do too.)

Practice. Make some space in your life for confession, discipleship, and accountability (i.e., a small group of committed friends with whom you can grow in God).

CHAPTER EIGHT

FAMILY TIES

The time came for the Jewish Festival of Tabernacles.
So Jesus's brothers approached him.
"Leave this place," they said, "and go to Judaea! Then
your disciples will see the works you're doing. Nobody who
wants to become well known does things in secret. If you're
doing these things, show yourself to the world!"
Even his brothers, you see, didn't believe in him.

—JOHN 7:2-5

An ancient burial box inscribed "James, son of Joseph, brother of Jesus"
was discovered in a private antiquities collection in Israel in 2002. The
stone box bearing the inscription is called an ossuary.

In ancient Palestine, particularly in the first century, an ossuary (or
"bone box") was one part of a two-stage burial process. The deceased
person's body was first laid in a tomb, then after a year or so the skeletal
remains were carefully collected and placed in an ossuary.*

---

* Two of the most famous ossuaries or bone boxes discovered from this period provide
a rare glimpse into practices and people from New Testament times. The first, found in
1968, bears the inscription "Yehohanan, son of Hagakol." Inside the ossuary is a heel bone
which has an iron stake driven through it, evidence that this man was crucified.

The second ossuary, discovered in 1990, features the name Caiaphas and contains the
bones of a sixty-year-old man. Because the carving on the box is especially ornate and also
because of another name included in the inscription, some scholars believe this ossuary
may well contain the bones of the high priest Caiaphas, who oversaw the arrest and trial
of Jesus (John 11:49–50).

While there's a great deal of debate as to whether the Aramaic inscription "James, son of Joseph, brother of Jesus" is a modern forgery (and most experts think it is), what the discovery has highlighted is the age-old question of whether Jesus of Nazareth had siblings.

For various and critical reasons, Catholic, Orthodox, and Protestant theologians are divided on that issue. For example, when the gospel accounts refer to the brothers and sisters of Jesus (e.g., Mark 6:3):

- Are they referring to Joseph's children from a previous marriage? (Joseph, in this view, was a widower before he was married to Mary.)
- Are they referring to Jesus' cousins? (One way of reading the text suggests that alternative.)
- Or are the brothers and sisters Jesus' blood relations, half-brothers and half-sisters whom Joseph and Mary had together later?

Regardless of where you land on that enduring issue, we must keep in mind that Jesus most certainly had family members in his life who were just like siblings to him.

MY BROTHER AND SISTER, WHO ARE BOTH OLDER THAN ME, are named Tré and Krista. We each have families of our own now, and we all live in different places, but the three of us remain unusually close in our respect and affection for one another.

That wasn't always the case, especially between my brother and me. Even though Tré and I are as thick as thieves now, there was a time when I didn't know if my brother and I would be able to reconcile our differences.

Siblings can butt heads in the most fierce and foolhardy of ways. I think one of the reasons why is that brothers and sisters have a unique perspective on each other's strengths and weaknesses.

My brother, Tré, and I are similar in some ways and quite different in others. For a few years—and I think it was more my fault than his—the crux was that we were trying to force the other into our own image.

To put it more plainly: I wanted Tré to be more like me.

I wanted him to see the world the way I did. I wanted him to respond to certain issues like I did. I wanted my brother to acknowledge that my way was right, his way was wrong, and that was that.

There's really no way around it: I acted like an arrogant jerk.

Thankfully, because of the prayers (and tears) of our family and through the wise, professional counsel of a close friend named Rod Smith, my brother and I found peace. Our friendship was fully restored. Incredibly, it's better than ever.

Sure, it took us awhile to get there, because most important journeys take time, but we made it, and I'll never forget one of the turning points. It was a symbolic act suggested by our sage mother.

Tré and I took a used diaper (his daughter Elena was just a baby at the time), we dug a deep hole in the ground, and then—with some tears and laughter—my brother and I buried that stink beneath a load of earth.

The diaper and its contents were meant to represent all of the hurtful things we had thought, said, and done to each other during that painful season, and, wow, I can't tell you how good it felt to get rid of that soiled mess.

When it comes to family ties, especially those that have been severely strained and even broken, you can't always figure out each and every part of what went wrong. Sometimes, you've just got to cover it with a whole lot of love instead.

JAMES IS CALLED THE "BROTHER OF OUR LORD" IN THE NEW Testament, but he's mentioned only a few times. In Matthew and Mark, he is referenced by name. In the gospel of John, on the other hand, James is never called out directly, but it's safe to assume he was one of

"Jesus' brothers" who, according to the author, "didn't believe" in Jesus during a critical stretch of his ministry (7:5).

What's more, even when Jesus is being crucified, James and the other brothers are nowhere to be found, which might be one of the reasons why Jesus entrusts the care of his mother to another (John 19:26–27).

There's no further mention of James in the New Testament narrative until he shows up much later in the book of Acts. At which point, in a surprising turn of events, James has emerged as one of the primary leaders of the rapidly growing Jesus movement (Acts 12:17; 15:13).

The obvious question is when did James make peace with his brother Jesus?

Unfortunately, the Bible doesn't say, but the apostle Paul provides us with an interesting clue. In his first letter to the Corinthians, Paul quotes from the earliest Christian creed we have, a creed passed on to him by others, which claims that after Jesus was crucified and raised from the dead, he "was seen by James" (1 Cor. 15:3–8).

It's impossible to know, of course, what took place between Jesus and James in that significant resurrection encounter, but I have a feeling that those two brothers—who knew each other so well—took care of some important things that had once divided them.

I can't help but wonder whether Jesus told James something similar to what my older brother once told me: "Don't worry, it's all covered now."*

Ponder. Jesus knows how hard it can be when family bonds are strained to the point of breaking, particularly with those for whom we care so deeply.

---

* In case you're wondering what happened with Jesus' other siblings, Acts 1:14 suggests that at some point after the resurrection, they too were reconciled with their brother Jesus.

Pray. Pray for a family member who feels far away.

Practice. If you need help in healing a deep family wound, something that cannot be covered, then make an appointment to speak with a trained counselor or a pastor about it.

PART TWO

JESUS AND ABBA

"You are my son, my dear son! I'm delighted with you."
—LUKE 3:22

CHAPTER NINE

SELF-AWARE

*Jesus' parents used to go to Jerusalem every year for the
Passover festival. When he was twelve years old, they went
up as usual for the festival. When the feast days were over,
they began the journey back, but the boy Jesus remained in
Jerusalem. His parents didn't know . . .*

—LUKE 2:41–43

At what point does a child become an adult? When, exactly, does that
critical transition take place?

How we answer that question, of course, depends on when, where,
and to whom we ask it. If you asked that question to an eleven-year-old
boy working in a London textile factory in eighteenth-century England,
for example, you'd probably get a different answer than if you asked the
same question to an eighteen-year-old woman applying for university
in twenty-first-century America.

Economics, geography, skin color, timeframe, gender—all of it
shapes our understanding of what childhood and adulthood mean.

Important for us to understand is that the concept of teenager is
relatively recent. In the first century that phase between childhood and
adulthood was not a part of most people's experience.

What many people did experience, though (and in many cultures
still do), was a ceremonial coming of age, a symbolic rite of passage that

marked their transition from child to adult. To this day many Jewish people celebrate a bar or bat mitzvah service to recognize this formative period in a young person's life.

Bar means "son," *bat* means "daughter," and *mitzvah* means "commandment." The main idea of a bar/bat mitzvah service is that a boy or girl, at about the age of twelve or thirteen, officially becomes a "son or daughter of the commandment." Up until that point, it's understood that the parents are primarily responsible for their child's choices. After they have reached this critical age, the boy or girl is accountable for their own actions.

Taking all of that into account, it seems significant that the one story we have from Jesus' childhood takes place when "he was twelve years old" (Luke 2:42), a typical age in Jewish culture for a young person to become increasingly self-aware—which, apparently, is what was happening with Jesus.

SO WHAT EXACTLY DID JESUS KNOW ABOUT HIS IDENTITY and when did he know it? To put it plainly, only God knows.

But what the gospel of Luke does make clear is that by the time Jesus is about twelve years old, he is beginning to identify with the God of his people in a unique and intimate way.

We'll pick up Luke's story at the point when Mary and Joseph, after feverishly searching for their son over a three-day stretch in Jerusalem, find him at last:

> And so it happened that after three days they found him in the Temple, sitting among the teachers, listening to them and asking them questions. Everyone who heard him was astonished at his understanding and his answers.
>
> When they saw him they were quite overwhelmed.
>
> "Child," said his mother, "why did you do this to us? Look—your father and I have been in a terrible state looking for you!"

"Why were you looking for me?" he replied. "Didn't you know that I would have to be getting involved with my father's work?" They didn't understand what he had said to them. (Luke 2:46–50)

One of the most unusual parts of this passage is that twelve-year-old Jesus seems genuinely surprised that his parents don't understand what he's up to: "Why were you looking for me?" he asks Mary and Joseph. "Didn't you know that I would have to be getting involved with my father's work?" (And when he refers to his father here, Jesus doesn't mean Joseph.)

Think about what Jesus is asking: Didn't you know?

Didn't you know this day would come?

Didn't you understand, Mom and Dad, my path would lead me here?

Didn't you realize I would discover an identity and calling uniquely my own?

And think about the revealing way Luke describes Mary and Joseph's bewildered response: they didn't understand.

It really is an arresting thought. Because, maybe, for the first time in his life—here in the Temple courts, when he is twelve years old—Jesus is realizing that he knows and understands some things that his parents don't.

MORE THAN A THOUSAND WORDS IN THE GOSPEL ACCOUNTS come directly from Jesus, but the only words we have from his childhood are these:

"Why were you looking for me? Didn't you know that I would have to be getting involved in *my father's work*?" (Luke 2:49, italics added).

While it wasn't unheard of in ancient Jewish culture to refer to God as Father (see, for example, Deut. 32:6 or Isa. 64:8), the title is always used in reference to the Hebrew people as a whole. It was a communal title.

What's groundbreaking about the way Jesus uses this name for

God is the personal way he says it—my father. Jesus uses the title in a possessive and singular sense, as if he belongs to the Father, and the Father belongs to him.

This intimate, vulnerable interaction between Jesus and God comes out even more clearly in a desperate moment of prayer shortly before Jesus is crucified:

"Abba, Father," he said, "all things are possible for you! Take this cup away from me! But—not what I want, but what you want" (Mark 14:36).

The word Abba here is the Aramaic word for Father, and Aramaic, mind you, was most likely Jesus' mother tongue.

Much has been made of the childlike meaning behind the word Abba, that it might mean, for example, something like "Daddy" or "Papa." In Aramaic, though, Abba is the only word there is for Father or Daddy or Papa.

All of those sentiments of intimacy, respect, even awe are wrapped up in that one simple word, Abba.

The important point, we must understand, is not whether Jesus specifically meant Father, Papa, or perhaps even just Dad when he said Abba. The important point is that Jesus talked with God in the close, personal way that a child talks with a beloved parent—and, yes, that was highly unusual, a point we will explore later.

Perhaps equally unusual is the fact that just at the point when young Jesus claims to be getting involved in his father's work, he promptly returns home to Nazareth for the next eighteen years of his life— eighteen years, remember, of which we know next to nothing.

The gospel of Luke, it seems, tells the narrative like this intentionally, leaving us with that singular, mysterious image of twelve-year-old Jesus in the Temple, a boy on the verge of becoming a man, alone in his deep and abiding understanding of what it means that God is Abba.

There's an important lesson here for us all: long before Jesus went public with his ministry, he was practicing a deep, personal, close connection with Abba Father in his day-to-day, ordinary human experience.

Ponder. After this one unusual episode at age twelve, it is not until Jesus is thirty years old that we meet him again. The eighteen years in between are "hidden."

Pray. Ask that you, like Jesus, will be about the Father's work in your day-to-day, ordinary responsibilities: attending school, parenting children, going to work.

Practice. Take stock of your daily routines and particularly your relationships: Are you the same person in public that you are in private?

CHAPTER TEN

SECOND

*Very early—in the middle of the night, actually—Jesus got
up and went out, off to a lonely place, and prayed.*
—MARK 1:35

I still remember the first time I found my wife praying, the impact it
made on me. Even now, more than fifteen years later, I can still see
the tears on her face.

It was before we were married, when Bronwyn and I were students
at Wheaton College. I was twenty-six years old, immersed in graduate
studies, and prone to take myself a bit too seriously. Bronwyn was
nineteen, midway through her second year of undergrad, and she wore
the most marvelous silver ring in her nose.*

We met while I was taking an evening class about the life and times
of Jesus. The class was being held in Blanchard Hall, next door to the
campus coffeehouse, aka the Stupe. Bronwyn worked at the Stupe
part-time, and during a break in lecture, I strolled over to grab a quick
snack before returning to Dr. Elwell's class.

Bronwyn was serving behind the counter that night, and through
a providential chain of events, particularly because she was a math

---

* Yes, there are seven years between us, which is one of the reasons I planned an
elaborate celebration when Bronwyn turned twenty, because it meant that I was no longer
dating a teenager.

minor at the time, she mistakenly shortchanged me five cents for a Peppermint Patty.

Counting the coins in my hand (I was a miserly grad student, what can I say?), I looked up to point out the discrepancy, and it was then, at that moment, that I actually saw Bronwyn for the first time.

Three things hit me all at once. Her long hair was henna-dyed to a deep violet-red. That silver ring in her nose, beautifully and fiercely feminine, looked like it was meant to be there. And finally, "Bronwyn," written in cursive on her nametag—it sounded ageless to me. (And it's quasi-Tolkienian too, isn't it?)

Bronwyn quickly realized what had happened, laughed a little about shortchanging me, and then kindly handed over that oh-so-important five cents. I stood in line for just a moment more, staring, and then, without saying a word, made my way back to Blanchard Hall.

But I wasn't listening to Dr. Elwell's lecture anymore.

And I certainly wasn't thinking about Jesus.

It took me two more months of trips to the Stupe and "randomly" running into Bronwyn on campus before I worked up the courage to ask her out on a proper date. Thankfully, she said yes.

A few months into our dating relationship, I dropped by the Stupe to see her. One of Bronwyn's coworkers told me she had left early that day and was probably in the little prayer chapel nearby.

I walked through the chapel doors and found Bronwyn on her knees, praying. She had no idea I was there.

When Bronwyn looked up at last, I could see tears streaming down her face. But it wasn't her tears that impacted me so profoundly. It was the peace in her countenance, a deep well of God-trust in those tear-filled eyes.

I came to understand something important about Bronwyn in that moment. Regardless of where our relationship led, at best, I would always be second in her life.

IT IS VIRTUALLY IMPOSSIBLE TO SEPARATE JESUS FROM HIS prayer life. Truly, it's that core to who he is. Each of the gospel writers comments on it:

- "After he had sent the crowds away, Jesus went up the mountain by himself to pray" (Matt. 14:23).
- "Very early—in the middle of the night, actually—Jesus got up and went out, off to a lonely place, and prayed" (Mark 1:35).
- "It happened around that time that Jesus went up into the mountain to pray, and he spent all night in prayer to God" (Luke 6:12).
- "After Jesus had said this, he lifted up his eyes to heaven . . . 'Father, I want the ones you've given me to be with me where I am'" (John 17:1, 24).

When you read about Jesus' prayer life, the intimate and ongoing way in which he interacted with Abba Father, you don't get the sense Jesus is operating from a place of religious obligation. This isn't someone praying because it's the right thing to do. This is someone praying because he wants to, because praying is an essential part of who he is.

Although each of the descriptions of Jesus' all-nighters in prayer move me, it's that curious passage in the gospel of John that really gets me: "Father, I want the ones you've given me to be with me where I am."

Consider that strange request: "to be with me where I am."

What on earth is Jesus talking about?

Seriously, think about it: The disciples are already there, aren't they? They're standing right beside Jesus when he makes this request of the Father.

Apparently, Jesus is getting at something much more profound, something much more mindblowing than mere location when he asks the Father for his disciples "to be with me where I am."

What the gospel of John seems to be suggesting is that even

though Jesus was present with his disciples in this moment, Jesus was somehow—through prayer—present with the Father too.

And *that* is what he wants his disciples to experience:
fellowship, friendship, and presence of the Father,
the exact sort of thing that Jesus experiences in prayer.

FOR A LONG TIME, TO BE HONEST WITH YOU, I SECRETLY wished that prayer were not so central to following Jesus, because I didn't feel very good at it.

Prayer felt forced and obligatory. I would close my eyes tightly, do my very best to concentrate on God (and whatever I happened to be praying about that day), and then I would just *think harder.*

It was exhausting. It was annoying. It was maddening.

Far too many times, I must confess, I walked away from those moments more confused, frustrated, and upset than I was before. Prayer became a burden. It was something I should do, not something I wanted to do.

But when I read about Jesus praying, and when I watched Bronwyn praying, it was different. I didn't see religious obligation at work in Jesus and Bronwyn.

I saw fellowship, friendship, and presence, and *that* is what I wanted. Even though I didn't realize it at the time, I was desperate for it. I was desperate for the power of relationship to overthrow the tyranny of religion in my life.

I was desperate to pray from a place of desire instead of from a place of duty.

I was desperate to find peace in prayer, to wildly abandon religious obligation and to replace it with innocent, childlike trust: to know and experience what it means that God is close, that God is near, that God is Abba Father.

Ponder. Consider Jesus' words: "Father, I want the ones you've given me to be with me where I am." Is that your experience of prayer?

Pray. Ask that your eyes will be open to the wonder and welcome of prayer, that you'll be radically free of religious obligation and ready to embrace the presence of God.

Practice. If you can, find someone who prays without a hint of obligation and learn from them. (A wonderful resource is the British-based prayer movement 24-7prayer.com, and its accompanying prayer course, prayercourse.org.)[10]

CHAPTER ELEVEN

(ON AND ON)

There came a voice from heaven: "You are my son, my dear son! I'm delighted with you."
—LUKE 3:22

Humans seek acceptance through so many things—whether it's the friends we claim, the clothes we wear, or how much, how hard, or how little we work. We're almost hardwired for approval, aren't we?

I cannot count how many times my children have said to me something along the lines of, "Daddy, watch this!" It doesn't matter what it is—twirling in a circle, jumping off the top bunk, making a funny face in the mirror—my kids just want to be sure that I see them, that my eyes are on them, that what they're doing brings me as much joy as it brings them.

Little kids are quirky like that. They have no pretense about their human need for acceptance.

As we grow older, even though we all still long for that sort of approval, it's increasingly hard to know where to find it:

You make a new friend, but they let you down.
You get the promotion, but you hate the job.
You have the baby, but you're up all night.

And the beat goes on (and on and on).

Somewhere along the way you can't help but wonder:

Maybe I've missed it.

Maybe she/he is not the one.

Maybe I'm just not cut out for parenting.

Maybe I can find what I'm looking for somewhere else.

And the beat goes on (and on and on).

But what if there's another way?

What if Jesus knows how you feel?

What if the belonging you seek is much closer than you think?

JESUS' BAPTISM WAS A DEFINING MOMENT FOR HIM. IT WAS then that Jesus heard the words from heaven confirming his identity and clarifying his unique vocation, and it's important to consider the scene in full:

> So it happened that, as all the people were being baptized, Jesus too was baptized, and was praying. The heaven was opened, and the holy spirit descended in bodily form, like a dove, upon him. There came a voice from heaven: "You are my son, my dear son! I'm delighted with you." (Luke 3:21–22)

Before we unpack the rich, scriptural depth of what this scene reveals about (and perhaps even to) Jesus, let's first explore the raw physicality of it all.

There is Jesus—wet clothes clinging to olive-colored skin, his dark and unruly hair plastered against his forehead, water dripping from his chin as he looks skyward and sees:

There is Holy Spirit, in wild and soaring flight, coming down from above in the form of a dove, looking for a place to alight, a person to anoint, and then the voice from heaven is heard.

Yes, there is Abba Father—words deep like thunder, accepting and approving and affirming the Son, confirming within his soul what Jesus somehow already knows but still longs to hear:

"You are my son, my dear son! I'm delighted with you."

It really is a remarkable scene, isn't it? So remarkable that each of the gospel writers highlights it as a turning point in Jesus' journey. It's as if they want us to know: things were different after the baptism, and Jesus knew it.

So what did those weighty words from the Father mean, and how would Jesus have understood them in relation to his life, identity, and calling?

LIKE MOST DEVOUT JEWS OF HIS TIME, JESUS WAS IMMERSED in the holy scriptures. And it's in these scriptures, the narrative and history of the Hebrew people, the poetry and prophecy of the Jews, that Jesus confirms his deepest identity.

If you listen carefully to the iconic words at his baptism—"You are my son, my dear son! I'm delighted with you"—you will hear echoes of at least two ancient passages that would have come to Jesus' mind in this moment:

- From the book of Psalms: "I will tell of the decree of the LORD: He said to me, 'You are my son; today I have begotten you'" (2:7).
- From the prophet Isaiah: "Here is my servant, whom I uphold, my chosen, in whom my soul delights; I have put my spirit upon him . . ." (42:1).

There are all sorts of opinions as to how Jesus came to understand his identity and calling, but I am convinced that it was a journey that led him there, a journey of faith and discovery shaped primarily by three things:

1. the stories about his birth,
2. the unusual relationship in prayer he shared with Abba,
3. and the Hebrew scriptures in which he was immersed.

British theologian and Old Testament scholar Christopher Wright insightfully explains it like this:

> The answers came from his Bible, the Hebrew scriptures in which he found a rich tapestry of figures, historical persons, prophetic pictures and symbols of worship. And in this tapestry, where others saw only a fragmented collection of various figures and hopes, *Jesus saw his own face*. His Hebrew Bible provided the shape of his own identity.[11]

It seems the events surrounding Jesus' baptism provided the final pieces of the puzzle, affirming his identity and piecing together the unique and mysterious aspects of his calling.

As he watched the dove descend and felt the Spirit "upon him," Jesus heard in the voice of his Father prophetic echoes of ancient promises: the promise of a kingly son of the Lord who would inherit the nations (Psalm 2), the promise of a chosen servant, in whom the Father delights, who would suffer and die for his people, but who would be vindicated in the end (Isaiah 42–55).

The time was here at last. Jesus knew exactly what he was called to do.

IN THE PERSON OF JESUS, WE ENCOUNTER SOMEONE WHOSE identity and calling were not in competition. He lived and played, wept and worked from a deep and abiding knowledge of who he was: the dear son of the Father.

Like you and me, Jesus was faced with the frightening alternative of trying to find his identity in something less than the love of God. It's a deeply *human* temptation, isn't it? Because each and every one of us longs to be loved, to know that we belong, to know there is a place for us at the table, a place for us in the family, which is part of what Jesus, the dear son of the Father, came to accomplish on our behalf.

With his identity and calling now clearly laid out before him, it's as if you can almost hear Jesus whisper in response, "Abba, watch this!"

Ponder. What are some things, both good and bad, through which we seek acceptance, approval, and affirmation?

Pray. Ask that you would discover the deep, rooted identity of what it means to be loved, honored, and celebrated by the God whom Jesus calls Abba.

Practice. Make it a habit to affirm your friends and family. Tell them what you love, appreciate, and admire about them.

CHAPTER TWELVE

HUNGRY

Jesus returned from the Jordan, filled with the spirit. The spirit took him off into the wilderness for forty days, to be tested by the devil. He ate nothing during that time, and at the end of it he was hungry.

—LUKE 4:1–2

You can't help but laugh at Luke's understated style in this gem of a sentence: "He ate nothing during that time, and at the end of it he was hungry."

The gospel of Matthew makes the same point, but Matthew does so in a slightly different way: "He fasted for forty days and forty nights, and at the end of it was famished" (Matt. 4:2).

Famished sounds a bit more like it.

Because seriously, when you haven't eaten for forty days, you're not just hungry, you're ready to eat boiled rocks.

If you've ever fasted food for a significant period of time—or if you've just not had enough to eat because of some hardship—you'll understand what the gospel writers are getting at when they describe what Jesus was feeling like after he had not put food in his mouth for forty days. He was a very hungry man.

Think about it: it's not as if Jesus was given some sort of divine pass on certain aspects of his humanity, was he? No, of course not. Jesus hungered and thirsted, grew tired and became weary, needed to stretch his frame when he woke up in the morning, and experienced the process of aging just like we all do.

And that's important to keep in mind as we take these next three chapters to explore Jesus' forty days of fasting in the wilderness.

I ONCE FASTED FOOD A FULL FOUR WEEKS. (IT WAS ACTUally twenty-seven days, but who's counting? Okay, I was. Every single day.)

Here's a little of what I learned about our bodies along the way:*

- Your breath can smell pretty bad when you're fasting, especially during those first few days when your body is releasing a lot of stored up toxins. (Hint: drink more liquid to deal with that dry mouth.)
- The start of an extended fast can be physically challenging, and you may feel that challenge in particular during the first three to five days. (Hint: the intense hunger and occasional headache will probably pass after a few days, but they may well return with a vengeance toward the end.)
- Fasting with just water is more difficult than fasting with water and juice. (Hint: try including pure juices first, and then try with water alone later.)
- Once you've made it past those first few days of intense hunger and your body redirects its energies away from digestion, you may discover that your physical and mental reflexes significantly increase. (Hint: use this to your advantage by catching flies with your bare hand.)
- Finally, when it's time to break a fast, reintroduce foods slowly,

---

* I should mention that I am not a doctor, I am not an expert in fasting, and these statements have not been evaluated by the FDA. (There was no need to include that FDA caveat. I've just always wanted to write something that included that sort of thing, because it sounds so conspiratorial.)

and start with mild stuff that won't wreak havoc on your digestive tract. (Hint: don't ever break an extended fast by eating five oranges—acid overload!—all at once. My dad did that and it landed him in the hospital.)

I am drawing such detailed attention to the bodily effects of fasting because I believe it can help us better understand and identify with Jesus' humanity. For example:

- Jesus' breath probably smelled pretty bad during the first few days of his forty-day fast, especially when you take into account that water may not have been easily accessible in the wilderness.
- The hunger pangs hit Jesus the hardest at the beginning of his fast, eased midway through, and then returned with full effect toward the end of his forty days, when his body began to insist that without food he would die.
- This was not Jesus' first foray into fasting as a spiritual discipline. (One does not begin fasting with a forty-day nothing-but-water fast.)
- With Jesus' body less focused on digesting food, Jesus' mental acuity and awareness of his surroundings exponentially increased, in some ways making it the ideal time for him to be tested by the devil.
- While there is no record of what Jesus ate at the end of his forty days, there can be no doubt his digestive tract was seriously affected by it. His stomach rumbled and gurgled and probably even complained as those delicious morsels of food were welcomed back into his body at last.

FASTING IS AN ANCIENT PRACTICE THAT PURIFIES THE BODY, sharpens the mind, and holistically teaches us about dependence on

God. Moses did it, Elijah did it, and, following their examples, Jesus did it too.

What is unique about Jesus' forty days of fasting, though, is that, unlike Moses' and Elijah's fasts, it was not necessarily supernatural or miraculous.

For example, the Bible describes Moses' experience of fasting like this: "He was there with the LORD forty days and forty nights; he neither ate bread nor drank water" (Ex. 34:28). Without supernatural intervention, Moses could not have survived forty days without water.

Likewise, it is only after the prophet Elijah had eaten a miraculous meal that was prepared for him by an angel that "he went in the strength of that food forty days and forty nights" (1 Kings 19:8). That angelic food had some special, hidden ingredients.

But Jesus' fast was different.

Apparently, Jesus fasted like the rest of us.

He kept himself hydrated, he ate no food, and he endured.

It's critical to keep this in mind—that Jesus fasted like you and me—lest we find ourselves operating out of two possible extremes when it comes to fasting.

On the one hand, there's the tragic, true example of an old Zimbabwean man who died in 2015 attempting to emulate Jesus' forty days of fasting in the wilderness.[12] This devout man was under the impression that Jesus fasted without water. When the man tried to do the same, he died.

On the other hand, there's this typical and telling statement from a young American in his online article "Diary of a Forty-Day Fast": "My favorite part of the day is licking the peanut butter off the spoon after I scoop it into my protein shakes."[13] (Hate to break the news to you, brother, but that's actually drinking a meal.)*

---

* There is nothing wrong, of course, with including smoothies and protein shakes in a fast, but keep a couple of things in mind if you do: (1) a smoothie or shake is liquefied food (different from just juice or water), and (2) because your body is still consuming food, your digestive tract will still be active, and, unfortunately, your hunger pangs will follow suit.

The way Jesus fasted was different from these extremes, wasn't it? For Jesus, fasting was a regular, healthy, and practical part of his spiritual journey, one of the numerous ways in which he interacted with the God he called Abba. It strengthened his sense of identity, prepared him for the next phase of his calling, and enabled him to face the devil with a mind that was uncluttered and free.

How much more might it do for us?

Ponder. What are some other things (not just food) that you might choose to fast from for a time to learn greater dependence on God? (For example, I periodically fast internet news and social media.)

Pray. Ask that if you choose to fast, it will be from a place of simple devotion, not obligation.

Practice. If you have never fasted food before, maybe try it for one meal or perhaps even a full day. And, seriously, do seek medical advice if you are concerned about harmful side effects.

CHAPTER THIRTEEN

IF YOU ARE

Then the tempter approached him.
"If you really are God's son," he said . . .
—MATTHEW 4:3

The gospel writers are clear that Jesus did not spend six weeks in the wilderness on a whim. No, he was there for a reason: "to be tested by the devil" (Matt. 4:1; Mark 1:13; Luke 4:2).

The accounts are equally clear as to how Jesus was guided into this time of intense testing: he was led there by "the spirit" (Matt. 4:1; Mark 1:12; Luke 4:1).

There are two important things to keep in mind as we explore this showdown in the wilderness.

First, the gospel writers have already introduced us to "the spirit" at Jesus' baptism, "coming down like a dove onto him" (Mark 1:10). This dovelike imagery is probably meant to remind us of how the Holy Spirit was "hovering" or "brooding" like a bird over creation at the dawn of time (Gen. 1:2).

With similar imagery, like a mother bird urging her young out of the nest, the Spirit is now leading Jesus into his destiny, into the vocation for which he was born. The time is here at last for the dear son of the Father to spread his wings and fly.

Second, for the first time in the gospel writings, we are introduced to "the devil," an age-old enemy that Jesus will encounter in multiple ways throughout his ministry. (In the gospel records, the devil is also referred to as the accuser, the tempter, or the strongman.)

The introduction of the devil should again take our minds back to Genesis, when a prehistoric foe in the form of a deadly serpent deceived Adam and Eve, the mother and father of the human race, into sinning against God, betraying their original design as image-bearers of the Creator. But this time, with *this* human, things will be different.

With that epic and ancient framework in mind—the Holy Spirit urging Jesus into his destiny, and the deceiving serpent just waiting for the perfect time to strike—let's now consider the title by which the devil addresses Jesus: "God's son."

CERTAIN TITLES HAVE LEVELS OF MEANING AND, AS A result, can sometimes be a little confusing. "God's son" is that sort of title.

Let me explain.

A dear friend of mine named Tim is a devoted father of three children, and he is also an Anglican priest. Depending on the context that Father Tim is in, whether he's with his family at home or with his parishioners at church, the title Father has different meanings, doesn't it?

If you asked me, "Trent, is your friend Tim a good father?" I would answer, "Yes," but I might be a bit confused about which meaning of the word father you have in mind.

A similar confusion can surround the well-known title "God's son" when used in reference to Jesus. Because that title, in its first-century setting, was loaded with multiple levels of meaning that might not be evident to you and me:[14]

1. It could mean the Hebrew people as a whole, who are described as God's "firstborn son" in Exodus 4:22.
2. It could mean the anointed king, the coming conquering Messiah, who is described by the word of the LORD as a

"son" in 2 Samuel 7:12–14. (For clarity's sake, it's important to note that "God's son" was most commonly understood in this sense—as a human, political title—before it was seen in new light through the life, death, resurrection, and ascension of Jesus.)

3. It could mean the Son of the Divine, a title used in reference to Roman emperors and engraved on Roman coins, like the coin in Luke 20:20–26.
4. And finally, "God's son" could mean, as it does in some early Christian writings, "the image of God, the invisible one, the firstborn of all creation. For in him all things were created . . ." as it says in Colossians 1:12–20.

If you were to ask the gospel writers, "Is Jesus the Son of God?" they would undoubtedly answer, "Yes," but they might have various levels of meaning in mind.

1. Yes, Matthew 1:1 would say, Jesus is the ultimate "son of Abraham," and he represents the Hebrew people as a whole.
2. Yes, Mark 14:61 would say, Jesus is "the Messiah, the Son of the Blessed One," the now and forever anointed King of the Jews.
3. Yes, Luke would say in Acts 17:7, there is indeed "another king, Jesus," and he (not Caesar) is the true and rightful ruler of the world.
4. And yes, John 1:1–14 would say, Jesus was "in the beginning . . . the Word. The Word was God . . . the Word became flesh . . . the father's only son . . ."

The gospel writers are unanimous: "Yes, Jesus is the Son of God!" But while for us this seemingly straightforward title might exclusively mean the "second person of the Trinity," it carried a richer, more layered meaning in its first-century context.

SO WHEN THE DEVIL SAYS TO JESUS, "IF YOU REALLY ARE God's son," what does he mean by that title? Did this deceiving, ancient foe truly understand the divine identity of the one with whom he was dealing in the wilderness?

At least during this showdown, I am not convinced he did. The reason I think this is fairly straightforward: the most common understanding of the title "God's son"—*before* it is radically reinterpreted through the life, death, resurrection, and ascension of Jesus—primarily meant Messiah in a human, political sense and not so much in a divine sense. If that's how most people—even Jesus' disciples—understood the title before it was loaded with new layers of meaning in Jesus, why should the devil be any different? After all, the devil is not omniscient. So this makes me suspect that perhaps he didn't grasp the full extent of who he was really dealing with that day. (Feel free to disagree with me, of course.)

When the devil says to Jesus, "If you really are God's son," I think what he means by the title "God's son" is Messiah—in a primarily human, political sense. And there were numerous candidates for the political role of Messiah in Jesus' day.

For example, according to first-century Jewish historian Josephus, there was a contemporary of Jesus named Theudas, who was called Messiah—or, in Greek, Christ. This would-be Christ, Josephus explains, was captured by the Romans and decapitated in Jerusalem.

During this same era, Luke writes in the book of Acts, there was another would-be Messiah, Judas the Galilean, "who drew a crowd after himself. But he was killed, and all those who trusted him were scattered" (Acts 5:37).

Keeping in mind famous first-century figures like Theudas and Judas the Galilean, here's the important point: there were others claiming the Messiah title before (and after) Jesus, and there were other ways of understanding what the unique role of Messiah would be.

I think that is what is at issue in the temptations of Jesus: "If you really are God's son, the Messiah," the devil whispers, "then do what the people are expecting the Messiah to do—unleash holy fury on the Romans and establish the Temple as your center of power." (The ensuing chaos, the devil may have reasoned, would advance his own agenda of violence, suffering, and sorrow.)

As the gospel story unfolds, this messianic expectation is an ongoing issue for Jesus. The crowds, the disciples, even the devil in his own twisted way—they all want to mold Jesus according to their expectations.

But Jesus is having none of it. "At his temptation," explains Robert Stein in *Jesus the Messiah*, "Jesus settled once and for all the *kind* of Messiah he would be."[15]

And in some ways—at least as it relates to expectations—what Jesus experiences in the wilderness is an age-old temptation that each and every human must face: Will we be shaped by the expectations of others or by the expectations of God?

Ponder. One of the great temptations of Jesus' life was to live according to the expectations and hopes of others instead of the expectations and hopes of Abba Father.

Pray. Ask for courage, clarity, and confidence when you are faced with the choice of pleasing others or pleasing God—at work, at school, or at home.

Practice. Consider your greatest fear of what might happen if you choose to honor God in a challenging situation (i.e., an issue of integrity at work or school, or a moral decision in a relationship) and surrender that fear to God.

CHAPTER FOURTEEN

EAT, JUMP, BOW

When the devil had finished each temptation, he left him
until another opportunity.
—LUKE 4:13

I once heard a preacher label Luke 4:13 as the most sinister verse in the Bible, and I think he was right. The words almost drip with venom, don't they, and can't you just see that crafty, old serpent, embittered at losing the battle, slithering away to fight another day?

We know nothing as to what form the accuser took when he came tempting Jesus in the wilderness. Did he adopt the image of a primordial, whispering snake, like that one in the garden so long ago? Or perhaps he opted for a more traditional devil-like vibe this time round, replete with flaming horns, bloodstained claws, and scaly skin?

Both of those caricatures seem pretty far-fetched to me. Even more so when you take into account what the apostle Paul says in one of his earliest letters: "The satan himself transforms himself to look like an angel of light" (2 Cor. 11:14).

Read those words again, more slowly, letting the message burrow deep inside: "The satan himself transforms himself to look like an angel of light."

There is a vital truth here, one that Jesus knew all too well, and one that we must always, always keep in mind: evil takes various forms, and most dangerous of all is the evil that appears to be good.

WE NEED NOT COMPLICATE THE WILDERNESS STORY WITH symbolism, because the temptations of Jesus, when understood in context, are tangible. This is a story of politics and power, of what it means to be Messiah.

It's a story that is played out again and again in various spheres of influence, how leaders can rise to such glorious heights, carrying the hopes of so many as they do, and then when they fall from those glorious heights and some hidden evil is revealed, it affects us all.

Because we trusted that pastor or preacher.

Because we voted for that president or prime minister.

Because we believed, truly and deeply, in the power they claimed to represent.

Often in those situations if you can track the twisted history back to where it first unraveled, you'll discover three simple words behind it all:

Eat, jump, bow.

"I'll give you exactly what you want," the inviting voice says, "and in return all you have to do is jump when I say jump, and bow when I say bow."

So the devil comes tempting with food—"If you really are God's son, tell these stones to become bread!"—because after forty days of fasting, a bite to eat is exactly what Jesus wants (Matt. 4:3).

But the temptation is not just about what Jesus wants, it's also about what the people of first-century Palestine want in a Messiah. They want a leader who will help them provide food for their families, who will enable them to make a steady income, who will create a sense of stability in a world that so often feels like it's falling apart. And isn't that a good thing? Isn't that what we all want for our families and communities?

"'The Bible says,' replied Jesus, 'that it takes more than bread to keep you alive. You actually live on every word that comes out of God's mouth'" (Matt. 4:4, and Jesus is quoting Deut. 8:3).

No, he responds to this temptation, there is immeasurably more to being human than just skin and blood and bones, and Jesus will not be ruled by what his flesh most desires—in this case, something to eat.

Realizing that Jesus is not swayed the way so many leaders are, the devil then tempts him with power, urging Jesus to cash in on the amazing investment of power he has just been given by the Holy Spirit at his baptism.

> The devil took him off to the holy city and stood him on the pinnacle of the Temple. "If you really are God's son," he said, "throw yourself down. The Bible does say, after all, that 'God will give his angels a command about you'; and 'they will carry you in their hands, so that you won't hurt your foot against a stone.'" (Matt. 4:5–6)

Here the deceiver really begins to work his dark magic, quoting a passage of scripture from Psalm 91:11–12 about the coming king, the Messiah, and tempting Jesus to use God's power to his advantage. Surely a miraculous sign, taking place at the Temple, the seat of power in the holy city, would prove once and for all to the religious and political leaders exactly whom Jesus is—and, for what it's worth, wouldn't that be a good thing?

"'But the Bible also says,' replied Jesus, 'that you mustn't put the Lord your God to the test!'" (Matt. 4:7, and Jesus is quoting Deut. 6:16).

True power is meant to serve, not to perform, and Jesus will not manipulate his anointing for his own advantage. He will not be told when or where to *jump*.

By this point in the wilderness narrative, you get the sense the devil is becoming desperate, almost whispering aloud: "Who does this Jesus think he is? Does he not realize how many would-be Messiahs I have met in my time, how many have fallen before him? Does this fool from Nazareth not know of Yehudah Maccabeus, of Theudas the Christ, of Judas the Galilean? How dare he quote the scriptures to me!"

(By the way, I am not suggesting that these historical figures were tempted by the devil in the same way that Jesus was tempted. Rather, I'm noting that these figures sought to overthrow their foreign oppressors and accomplish God's will through violent military campaigns, which is exactly what the people—and perhaps even the devil—were expecting the Messiah to do.)

Enraged, the serpent unmasks himself:

> Then the devil took him off again, this time to a very high mountain. There he showed him all the magnificent kingdoms of this world.
>
> "I'll give the whole lot to you," he said, "if you will fall down and worship me."
>
> "Get out of here, you satan!" replied Jesus. "The Bible says, 'Worship the Lord your God, and serve him alone!'" (Matt. 4:8–10, and Jesus is quoting Deut. 6:13)

The devil has revealed his diabolical hand, it's worship he's after, and Jesus will never *bow* to him, not for all the kingdoms of this world.

YOU CAN'T MAKE A DEAL WITH THE DEVIL, REGARDLESS OF how good it seems to be. The deceiver may help you get exactly what you want, but whether or not he tells you, the terms of the deal will be devastating.

That's the problem with sin: it seems so appealing in the moment, but the devil is in the details, always.

Adam and Eve, the mother and father of humanity, were deceived into believing they could gamble against the love and wisdom of God. In effect, they went from Paradise to Sin City, pawned their inheritance for a handful of dirty cash, and threw the dice.

They put everything they had on the table, and they lost it—all of it—on a lie.

The serpent's terms were excruciating. Because from that moment on, every son and every daughter would be a slave to that lie, indebted to the devil, bound by the chains of our greatest fear: that God is not good, that God does not love us, that God cannot be trusted.

But what the devil didn't see coming was Jesus.

Because here, at long last, in the flesh of his ancestors, is a human who will not be bound by the lie. Here is the faith-filled descendant of Adam and Eve who will remain true to what humans were always meant to be: the beloved, accepted, image-bearing children of God.

No, the devil didn't see this one coming. He never bargained on the Son (1 Cor. 2:8).

Ponder. In the same way that the devil masquerades as an angel of light, temptation often masquerades as opportunity. Have you ever experienced that sort of temptation?

Pray. Ask that you will readily recognize the devil's voice when he comes whispering, "Eat, jump, bow," that you will not be swayed by temptation.

Practice. Make it a point, like Jesus, to fill your mind with the scriptures so you will know exactly what to tell the devil when he comes tempting—because he will.

CHAPTER FIFTEEN

REAL AUTHORITY

Jesus returned to Galilee in the power of the spirit. Word
about him went throughout the whole district. He taught in
their synagogues, and gained a great reputation all around.
—LUKE 4:14

When I was nineteen years old, I preached a sermon that most in attendance never forgot. Even now, some twenty years later, I occasionally come across people who were there, and they always remember exactly what I said.

I was pretty impressed with myself for being invited to speak in the first place. I had barely begun my undergraduate studies, yet here I was, already teaching others.

"My students" (that's what I liked to call them back then) were all young, like me, and the organizers of the conference invited me to deliver two sermons, one in the morning and one in the evening.

I cannot tell you how many hours I spent preparing those sermons. The first was about how God pursues us, the second about how we pursue God.

The morning's message went exactly as planned. I was funny at the beginning and fiery at the end. That was how I liked to roll: get the kids laughing, surprise them with how well you can relate, and then hit them hard with the weight of sin.

With the morning session having gone so well, I arrived for the evening session focused. My text that night was from one of Paul's letters to his student, Timothy, when he instructed the young man, "Run away from the passions of youth" (2 Tim. 2:22).

But the words—"run away"—seemed far too weak to me. So I decided to go with the much weightier, punchier King James Version, which puts it like this: "Flee youthful lusts."

The sermon was going amazingly well that night. I was in rare form, as fiery as ever, warning the kids left and right of the dangers and consequences of sin, my voice rising and falling to a pounding cadence of pure and unadulterated truth.

As I reached the climax of my sermon, preparing to cry aloud with the great apostle himself—"Flee youthful lusts!"—for a brief, flittering second my mind returned to the morning's message, where with similar passion I had cried, "God pursues his people!"

The result of confusing my sermons in that critical moment was cataclysmic. For with every ounce of my religious zeal bearing down upon them, I cried to that terrified congregation of teenagers, "Pursue youthful lusts!"

As the unexpected message rolled out of my mouth, it felt as if I was having an out-of-body experience. I desperately tried to stop myself, but it was too late.

The words landed with unthinkable impact and kids began literally falling from their seats in laughter. I do not exaggerate when I tell you the organizers of the event, tears streaming down their faces from the stupefying hilarity of my zeal, finally decided we had to take a fifteen-minute break before closing the meeting.

Truly, my words have never been forgotten.

JESUS WAS AN UNFORGETTABLE TEACHER TOO, BUT FOR different reasons. In a wildly inspiring episode that takes place just after the wilderness showdown with the devil, the gospel of Mark describes the start of Jesus' public ministry like this:

At once, on the sabbath, Jesus went into the synagogue and taught. They were astonished at his teaching. He wasn't like the legal teachers; he said things on his own *authority*.

All at once, in their synagogue, there was a man with an unclean spirit.

"What business have you got with us, Jesus of Nazareth?" he yelled. "Have you come to destroy us? I know who you are: you're God's Holy One!"

"Be quiet!" ordered Jesus. "And come out of him!"

The unclean spirit convulsed the man, gave a great shout, and came out of him. Everyone was astonished.

"What's this?" they started to say to each other. "New teaching—with *real authority*! He even tells the unclean spirits what to do, and they do it!"

Word about Jesus spread at once, all over the surrounding district of Galilee. (Mark 1:21–28, italics added)

What exactly is the gospel of Mark getting at when it says that Jesus taught with authority, what the writer later highlights as real authority?

At one level, the story is helping the reader understand that Jesus was not simply quoting what other teachers had said before him, like most of the legal teachers of that time did. No, this was new teaching, a way of reading and interpreting the Hebrew scriptures that was unique to Jesus.

But it wasn't simply what Jesus was teaching. It was what he was doing as well—in this case, casting out a demon.

This story in Mark comes shortly after the wilderness temptations, and it seems like Mark wants us to understand that Jesus is now taking the fight directly into the devil's domain—the domain of sin and sickness and suffering.

Almost immediately after this power encounter in the synagogue, Mark goes on to say, "When the sun went down and evening came, they brought to Jesus everyone who was ill, all who were demon-possessed. The whole town was gathered around the door" (Mark 1:32–33).

Word about the authority and power of Jesus was spreading, and for those who were there that first, extraordinary evening with him, for those who were set free and made whole, truly it was a night never to be forgotten.

JESUS, UNLIKE SOME THEOLOGIANS, DOES NOT VIEW GOD as the source of suffering. According to Jesus, the divine authority that he exercises, both in healing sickness and in forgiving sin, is a bold and open confrontation with the forces of evil at work in the world.

It's as if Jesus is announcing loudly and clearly to the powers that be, powers that have held humans captive to sin and sickness and sorrow for millennia now, "There's a new ruler in town, and your deceptive reign of fear and tyranny, sin and suffering is coming to an end."

As you might imagine, that kind of announcement, particularly when it's packed with that kind of punch, travels fast. The people, the leaders, even the demons come running. Everyone is trying to figure out just who this Jesus is.

The correct answer is now dawning on the demons: "What business have you got with us, Jesus of Nazareth? Have you come to destroy us? I know who you are: you're God's Holy One!" (Mark 1:24).

It's hard to say, of course, exactly what the demons mean by the title God's Holy One, but it's clear that they are now realizing they are dealing with an authority that seemingly comes from God alone.

"Be quiet!" Jesus orders the demon. "And come out of him!" (Mark 1:25).

Again, keep in mind the physicality of this encounter: this is not your Sunday school Jesus, meek and mild, sandy-blond hair blowing beautifully in the wind.

No, this is a first-century prophet, fiery and focused, rebuilding his physical strength after forty days of fasting food, veins bulging in his neck as he stares this demon down and, in effect, tells him:

You are not in charge here. I AM.

Ponder. Real authority is rooted in who you are—a child of God— and is best reflected in what you do, not just in what you say.

Pray. Ask for the grace and discipline of character to support your words with actions, that when you say, "I love you" to someone, for example, your actions will reflect your words.

Practice. Don't attempt to teach something you are not really living, because it might just backfire on you. The Father cares more about your character than your pride.

CHAPTER SIXTEEN

INTERVENTION

Jesus went into the house. A crowd gathered again, so they couldn't even have a meal. When his family heard it, they came to restrain him. "He's out of his mind," they said.
—MARK 3:20–21

Staging an intervention in a family member's life is incredibly challenging, maybe never more so than when that family member happens to be Jesus.

The stunning story of Jesus' family desperately trying to force some sense into him is one of the most raw and revealing moments in the whole of the gospel. Seriously, it's not at all what you would expect to happen.

In historical circles, this kind of thing is referred to as a criterion of embarrassment, which just means that this sort of story is presumed to be authentic because there would be no reason for the author to invent such an embarrassing account about Jesus and his family.

Imagine how this surprising scene unfolds:

- Jesus' reputation is spreading like wildfire, so much so that he barely has time to eat (Mark 3:20).
- As a result, "experts who had come from Jerusalem" are now in Galilee to try to discern what this emerging Jesus movement is all about, and their conclusion, because of certain things that

Jesus is saying and doing, is that he is "possessed by Beelzebul! He casts out demons by the prince of demons!" (Mark 3:22).

- Jesus' family, clearly aware of how dangerous it can be to cross the establishment and obviously worried about what Jesus is saying and doing, come "to restrain him" because, according to his family, Jesus is "out of his mind" (Mark 3:21).
- Finally, just in case we are unaware of the identity of this family (because, who knows, perhaps these are distant relatives who don't really know him), the gospel of Mark includes how the crowd describes the family to Jesus: "Your mother, your brothers, your sisters are outside! They're searching for you!" (Mark 3:32).

There is no mistake here: these are not distant relatives, people who don't really know Jesus. These are the people who apparently know Jesus best. These are the "brothers" and "sisters" Jesus grew up with, the ones he played with as a child on the dusty streets of Nazareth. These are his closest family members, including, we must understand, his very own mother, Mary.

FAMILY IS ONE OF GOD'S GREATEST GIFTS, WHICH IS WHY it can wound us so deeply. For better or for worse, family has the incredible capacity to hurt, to heal, to affirm, to abuse, to forgive, to inflict, to restore, to expose, to confuse, to clarify, to comfort, to frustrate, to lose, to love—and sometimes all in one day.

Jesus understands that. He really does. Because Jesus has family too. And it's complicated.

This unusual story in Mark's gospel does not conclude with Jesus and his family in a heated, public argument. Instead, it concludes with Jesus crying out to the crowds (and to his family as well), "Anybody who does God's will is my brother! And my sister! And my mother!" (Mark 3:35).

Let's be clear: Jesus' point here is not to wound his family, although I think he probably does.

Jesus' point here is to extend his family, because that's what he came to do.

This is part of what the writer of the book of Hebrews is getting at when Jesus is described as the elder brother of a brand-new family: "He isn't ashamed," the author explains, "to call them his brothers and sisters . . ." (2:11). The beautiful imagery used in this passage is a striking picture of the Son extending the love of the Father.

But, wow, for Mary and his siblings, when Jesus cries aloud during this intense interchange, "Who is my mother?" and "Who are my brothers?"—surely those words had to hurt. Like a wound in his siblings' heart or a sword in his mother's soul. Sometimes the truth hurts like that.

It was a sorrow well-intended, though, because Jesus—this elder brother, this firstborn son—was on a life and death mission to extend the family of God.

LET ME TELL YOU AN INCREDIBLE STORY ABOUT A SIXTY-something-year-old man named Justin, and what it means for him to be part of God's family in Jesus.

Justin was born in 1956 in London, England, to a mother and a father who were both alcoholics. Because of his parents' addictions, in Justin's own words, his "early life was messy."[16]

His parents divorced in 1959, when Justin was just three years old. While his mother, Jane, bravely decided to enter rehab in 1968, which led to the transformation in her life, unfortunately Justin's father, Gavin, died in 1977 because of alcoholism and smoking.

Justin's childhood was challenging, but he was blessed with a strong education, and he excelled at Eton College and at Cambridge University. After graduating from university and beginning a family, Justin went on to do well in the oil industry for eleven years before dramatically shifting direction and entering full-time preparation for Christian ministry with the Church of England.

The story of Justin's almost thirty years in ministry is much too long to tell here, but through an unusual chain of events, and much to the surprise of Justin himself, he was eventually appointed as the Archbishop of Canterbury in 2012.*

Justin's story does not stop there. On April 8, 2016, Archbishop Justin Welby released a personal statement explaining that he had just discovered that the man he always thought was his father was not his biological father.

For more than sixty years, Justin, his mother, and the man he thought was his father were all convinced he was a honeymoon baby. It turns out, though, that because of a brief affair, "fuelled by a large amount of alcohol," Justin's mother conceived him with another man just days before she was married.[17]

The archbishop broke the news in partnership with the *Telegraph*, the London newspaper that did all of the groundwork for the story. One of the reasons the paper was so interested in the story is because DNA testing revealed that Justin's biological father was a famous figure in British society, the late Sir Anthony Montague Browne, who was the last private secretary of Winston Churchill.

When the *Telegraph* reporter, Charles Moore, asked the archbishop if the news of his paternity made him revise or question his sense of self, Justin simply replied, "There is no existential crisis, and no resentment against anyone. My identity is founded in who I am in Christ . . . Genetics don't make any difference to this."[18]

The reporter then asked the archbishop if he had somehow found in God the father he lacked. "Yes!" Justin responded excitedly:

---

* For those unacquainted with that title, the Archbishop of Canterbury is the senior leader of the Church of England and the symbolic head of the worldwide Anglican Communion, which is the third largest Christian denomination in the world, representing more than 85 million people.

I thought it was [all] about forgiveness, repentance and new life, which are all very important. But finding in the midst of looking after my father that here was a Father who was perfectly dependable and utterly true and who knew me deeply and loved me much more certainly, was a surprise beyond belief . . .

Yes! This is the all-out wonder of what Jesus does for you and me. He makes a place for us in the family of God, just like he did for Archbishop Justin Welby.

Ponder. In Jesus, our genetics—"good" or "bad"—do not ultimately determine us.

Pray. Ask that you will know how much God loves you, and that regardless of your family background, challenges, and genetics, your true identity will be founded in Jesus.

Practice. Memorize this passage of scripture from Psalm 139: "For it was you who formed my inward parts; you knit me together in my mother's womb. I praise you, for I am fearfully and wonderfully made" (vv. 13–14).

PART THREE

JESUS AND HIS FRIENDS

*That's how Jesus came to be sitting at home with
lots of tax-collectors and sinners. They were
there, plenty of them, sitting with Jesus and his
disciples; they had become his followers.*
—MARK 2:15

CHAPTER SEVENTEEN

HIS COUSIN, OF COURSE

At that time, the word of God came to John, the son of Zechariah, in the wilderness. He went through all the region of the Jordan, announcing a baptism of repentance for the forgiveness of sins.
—LUKE 3:2–3

The stories of Jesus always start with John, as if this wild man in the wilderness was some sort of one-man demolition crew, boldly shouldering his way through the religious and political complexities of the first century to make way for Jesus.

And complex it was.

It was a turbulent time in ancient Palestine. Rome had invaded Jerusalem—the center of Jewish life and location of the Temple—some sixty years before Jesus was born. The entire region was now a strategic outpost of the Roman Empire, but there were wildly different responses to Roman rule:

- Some believed the only way to respond to Rome was through violence. About the time Jesus was born, there was a fierce uprising in the Palestinian region of Galilee. Roman soldiers brutally crushed that rebellion and then crucified two thousand Jewish rebels as a warning.

- Others thought the way to deal with Rome was via political compromise. This way of doing things was especially prevalent in a powerful group known as the Sadducees, who controlled the Temple in Jerusalem and benefitted greatly from the empire's taxation system.
- Still others, in response to compromise of that sort, were convinced the way to counter Rome's rule was through separation or exclusion. As a result, a significant "culture war" was taking place in ancient Judaism as to who was in and who was out of the people of God.

It was into this sort of charged religious-political setting that John the Baptist shows up in the Judean wilderness, dunking people in the River Jordan and "announcing a baptism of repentance for the forgiveness of sins" (Luke 3:3).

When we hear words like baptism and repentance and forgiveness, we subconsciously filter them through our modern sense of individualism, but the people of John's day would have heard those words differently.

For them, the idea of being baptized in the Jordan "was symbolically re-enacting what happened when the children of Israel came through the River Jordan and into the promised land," explains N. T. Wright in *The Original Jesus.* "It (was) all about . . . rescue, liberty, the new start that the people had longed for."[19]

No wonder vast crowds gravitated to John's wilderness movement, "questioning in their hearts whether John might not be the Messiah" (Luke 3:15).

Surprisingly, though, John redirects the increasing crowds to someone else: "I am baptizing you with water. But someone is coming who is stronger than I am. I don't deserve to untie his sandal-strap. He will baptize you with the holy spirit and with fire" (Luke 3:16).

John was talking about his cousin, of course, Jesus.

JOHN AND JESUS WERE BORN JUST A FEW MONTHS APART. While the gospel accounts do not reveal whether they ever interacted as children—oh, how I wish there was at least one story!—I think it's safe to assume that these two unique kids connected with each other at some point in their childhood.

Luke's gospel explains that their mothers, Mary and Elizabeth, were cousins, and that they spent significant time together during their pregnancies (1:36–56). Along with being relatives, Mary and Elizabeth shared the special bond of knowing that God had significant plans for their children. So it's not far-fetched to conclude that their sons crossed paths at festivals and family gatherings, maybe even numerous times.

A further clue as to the potential depth of Jesus and John's friendship comes in the gospel of Matthew, when Jesus follows the crowds to the River Jordan to be baptized by his longhaired, teetotaling, and increasingly well-known cousin.*

When Jesus steps into the Jordan, John tries to stop him: "I ought to be baptized by you," he says. "And are you going to come to me?" (Matt. 3:13–14).

There it is—in the tone of that deeply respectful question, you can sense the unusual bond these two share. Clearly, John and Jesus knew each other well.

I imagine it was partly because of that bond and understanding that John, at the high point of his popularity, hands over the reins of his movement to Jesus. *The Message* captures the nature of this significant leadership transition so well: "This is the assigned moment for him to move into the center," John says, "while I slip off to the sidelines" (John 3:30).

It was shortly after this, because of his fierce and public criticism of Herod, Rome's puppet ruler in Judea, that John the Baptizer was seized, put in prison, and, finally, beheaded. "His disciples came and

---

* Luke 1:15 seems to indicate that John was a lifelong Nazirite, meaning that among other things, he had vowed never to drink alcohol and never to cut his hair (Num. 6:1–21).

took away the body and buried it," records the gospel of Matthew. "Then they went and told Jesus" (14:12).

Jesus' response to this tragic news is telling: "When Jesus heard it, he went away from there in a boat to a deserted spot by himself" (Matt. 14:13).

JOHN'S DEATH HIT JESUS VERY HARD. ONE OF THE REASONS why is because Jesus felt things deeply. Again, the gospel records do not describe Jesus as an emotion-free, phantomlike figure floating through the first century. Quite the contrary, the portrait of Jesus in the gospel accounts reveals someone who experienced a full range of emotions:

- "When Jesus heard this he was astonished" (Luke 7:9).
- "He was deeply upset . . . and looked around at them angrily" (Mark 3:5).
- "Jesus looked hard at him, and loved him" (Mark 10:21).
- "Deeply stirred in his spirit . . . Jesus burst into tears" (John 11:33–35).
- "Then and there, Jesus celebrated in the holy spirit" (Luke 10:21).
- "And he hugged [the children] . . . and blessed them" (Mark 10:16).
- "When he came near and saw the city, he wept over it" (Luke 19:41).

All of these descriptions point to a person who is in touch with what is going on inside. I think this is one of the traits that so attracted people to Jesus. His feelings were not bottled up, pressed down, or hidden away. Jesus knew how to express what was happening in his heart, and he did, without shame.

That's why Jesus goes away to a "deserted spot" when he receives the news about John's death. Because when John died, Jesus lost more than a cousin. He lost a friend, a peer.

Jesus and John had thus far followed a similar trajectory in life and ministry:

- Both born via unusual circumstances (Luke 1:5–2:20).
- Both hidden away for a long season (Luke 1:80; 2:51).
- Both beginning their work at about age thirty (Luke 3:1–2; 3:23).
- Both announcing the coming of God's kingdom (Matt. 3:2; 4:17).

And now, in John's death, Jesus is most likely foreseeing what is on the horizon for him too. Even in his death, you see, John was leading the way for his dear cousin and friend Jesus.

In time there would be other close friends in Jesus' life (not least, the disciples), but I doubt any of them could ever take the place of his one-of-a-kind cousin and friend John.

Ponder. Do you have a peer-like figure in your life who urges you forward in your journey with Jesus, and have you told them how grateful you are for their friendship?

Pray. Ask that you, like Jesus, will know how to properly express what is happening inside, that your grief, your joy, and your frustration will not be bottled up or pressed down.

Practice. When it comes to areas you are grieving about, rejoicing about, or frustrated about, risk sharing those feelings with someone you trust and respect.

NICKNAMED

It happened around that time that Jesus went up into the
mountain to pray, and he spent all night in prayer to God.
When day came, he called his disciples, and chose twelve
of them . . .

—LUKE 6:12–13

When I was twenty-one years old, a close friend and I had the rare opportunity of spending most of a year traveling with and learning from Loren Cunningham, the founder of Youth With A Mission (YWAM).*

Loren is one of the most traveled people in history, having visited every sovereign nation on the planet, as well as numerous territories, enclaves, and island groups. One of the reasons Loren travels so widely is because, as the founder of a global mission organization, he feels called to preach the gospel in as many places as possible so that he can encourage others, especially young people, to "go into all the world" (Mark 16:15).

Judging from the scope of YWAM's ministry (which includes more than twenty thousand staff in eleven hundred locations in 180 nations), it certainly seems Loren's traveling and preaching is well on its way to having its desired effect.

---

* YWAM is a global movement of Christians from many cultures, age groups, and backgrounds dedicated to serving and following Jesus in a variety of ministries all over the world (ywam.org).

Loren is a man of tremendous vision, a vision truly global in its reach. But having spent a great deal of time traveling with, learning from, and carefully observing Loren, it's not necessarily the breadth of his vision that is most striking. It's his humility.

Let me give you an example.

I'll never forget when we were in Togo, West Africa, and Loren invited my friend Daniel and me to join him for a meeting with Togo's president of parliament.

Loren and the president were getting together for a personal meeting to discuss an educational initiative for the entire region. News cameras, high-ranking officials, and several key assistants surrounded the president upon our arrival.

But Loren, God bless him, had no entourage at all. Unless, of course, you count Daniel and me: both of us in our early twenties, standing as close to Loren as we could, and desperately trying to act as if we knew what we were doing.

Thankfully, the meeting went off without a hitch. Honestly, though, I can't help wondering whether Togo's president of parliament walked away that day thinking, "Why on earth did Loren Cunningham choose *those two* to come with him?"

IN THE ANCIENT WORLD IT WAS A SIGNIFICANT HONOR TO become a disciple or student of a well-known master-teacher like Jesus, and one of the most notable traits of Jesus' ministry is the unlikely disciples he chooses.

Here's a little of what we know about them:

First, most of the disciples knew who Jesus was, and Jesus knew them, before he called them to become his disciples.

One of the reasons we know this is because a number of them encounter Jesus while John the Baptizer is still ministering (John 1:35–45). Then after John is put in prison, Jesus, having observed them for some time, invites them to become his disciples (Matt. 4:12–22).

Jesus did not just randomly approach strangers and offer them an obscure invitation to "follow me." No, there is context to his invitation.

Second, a number of the disciples were already close friends.

Andrew and Peter, and James and John are two sets of brothers, and these four seem to be in some sort of fishing partnership with one another (Luke 5:9–10). There is also Philip, who is from Andrew and Peter's hometown, and Philip invites his friend Nathaniel to meet Jesus (John 1:44–46), and so on.

Jesus called the disciples to follow him *together*. One gets the feeling that Andrew and Peter, James and John, Philip and Nathanael, and probably a few of the others have already been dreaming and scheming together for some time.

Third, from what we can tell, none of the disciples come from a priestly or learned background.

Remember, Jesus' first disciples were mostly down-to-earth fishermen, the sort of guys who worked normal jobs. These were not scholarly ministers with advanced degrees. Even after Jesus' resurrection, mind you, the disciples are still being described as "untrained, ordinary men" (Acts 4:13).

And, finally, Jesus draws his disciples from diverse backgrounds.

Alongside the fishing foursome of Andrew, Peter, James, and John, Jesus also invites "Matthew the tax-collector" and "Simon the Zealot" to join his inner circle (Matt. 10:3; Luke 6:15). When you hear tax collector, think liberal and upper crust. When you hear zealot, think conservative and patriotic.

Once we take into account all of these dynamic personalities and backgrounds, it helps put into perspective why the gospel of Luke records that Jesus spent an entire night in prayer before "he called his disciples" (6:12–13).

Seriously, Jesus may have spent much of that night just asking the Father, "Abba, are you sure this is such a good idea? I mean, honestly, these guys might make a real mess of the movement."

I'VE NEVER MADE THIS PUBLIC BEFORE, BUT WHEN DANIEL and I were traveling with Loren, we coined a nickname for our dear friend and mentor: BDL.

Like YWAM, BDL is an abbreviation, and it stands for Big Daddy Loren. (Loren, what can I say? A book just seemed like the perfect place to reveal this beloved nickname both to you and to the world.)

Daniel and I chose the name BDL for two reasons:

First, because Loren Cunningham, more than any other person in recent history, has helped young people become involved in global mission work. Truly, he is the father (i.e., Big Daddy) of this unique and vital aspect of global Christianity.

Second, when Daniel and I coined the distinguished name BDL, we were both in our early twenties, and, at the time, it seemed like a perfectly reasonable idea.

Now, the reason I've told you about BDL is to tell you this: we give nicknames to people we like, to people we love, to people we know and genuinely appreciate.

What's amazing about the way Jesus interacted with his disciples is that apparently he gave some of them nicknames, new names, funny and affectionate titles that reflected what he saw in them (Matt. 3:1).

So Simon becomes Peter, which means "the Rock."

James and John become Boanerges, which means "Sons of Thunder."

And I wouldn't be surprised if there were other nicknames given as well.

Considering the unique and endearing relationship the disciples shared with their teacher, mentor, and friend, Jesus, I wouldn't be surprised if the disciples had a nickname for him too.

Ponder. A number of the disciples were already close friends before Jesus invited them to become his disciples. Jesus called them to follow him together.

Pray. Pray for your friends who are following Jesus and for those who are not.

Practice. Think about your close friends: Have you, like Philip with Nathanael, told them about your journey with Jesus?

SONS OF THUNDER
(AND THEIR MOM)

Then the mother of Zebedee's sons came up, with her sons,
to Jesus. She bowed low in front of him and indicated that
she had a special request to make.
"What do you want?" he asked her.
"It's about these two sons of mine," she said to him.
"Please say that, when you're king, they may sit, one at your
right hand and one at your left."
—MATTHEW 20:20–21

The gospels of Matthew and Mark disagree on something, and it's such a trivial and peculiar thing you would think the gospel writers would have at least sorted it out between themselves before they wrote their stories down.

The disagreement centers on an event that involves two of the disciples, James and John, whom Jesus has renamed, of course, the Sons of Thunder. According to the narrative, Jesus is asked if these two brothers could have the privilege of sitting at his right hand and left when he is crowned king.

But this is where the disagreement lies: Who, exactly, asked Jesus that question?

According to the gospel of Matthew, it was the mother of James and

John who asked it (20:20). According to the gospel of Mark, however, it was the brothers themselves who brought up this delicate matter with Jesus (10:35).

In biblical scholarship, this type of nitpicky disagreement over details is called the criterion of dissimilarity. Similar to the criterion of embarrassment, the criterion of dissimilarity helps to gauge the authenticity of ancient documents.

I know it may sound a little strange for dissimilarity to suggest authenticity, so let me explain.

If two versions of one story agree on the major points, but disagree on minor points, then according to the criterion of dissimilarity, it's likely that the story is true. The reason is that most people remember minor details of an event differently, and those minor differences in detail suggest authenticity.

So in this story about James and John, you get a sense that when Matthew reads Mark's account of what happened, he says, "Wait a second, Mark, I remember the story happening a little differently than that.

"It wasn't James and John who asked Jesus that question. It was their mom!"

And, wow, that little detail was probably something the Sons of Thunder would rather have kept under wraps, because that's just embarrassing.

WHEN I WAS PREPARING TO TRAVEL WITH LOREN CUNNING-ham (aka BDL), my mother helped me with lots of the planning details.

Our itinerary would take Loren, Daniel, and me to ten countries on three continents in six months, so on top of trying to figure out how to pay for such a trip (by working as a busboy at a pizzeria, cleaning swimming pools, and raising money through donors), I also had to figure out how to book a round-the-world ticket with a global airline alliance.

This was before online booking, and I was under the impression that if I could speak with just the right airline representative, I would find just the right ticket for just the right dates at just the right price. As a result, I made numerous phone calls to the same airline company.

Each time, I discussed with a different airline representative every part of Loren's itinerary, and each time, the representative came back to me with the same price, which was always more than I wanted to pay. I kindly thanked them, hung up the phone, and called the company again in a few minutes, always hoping to speak with just the right person.

Doing this for some time, I became increasingly frustrated. Kindly, my mother offered to make a few calls on my behalf. Soon, though, she came back with the same price that I had already been quoted.

What was I to do?

"Maybe I'm going about this the wrong way," I thought. "Next time, instead of talking about Loren's itinerary, I'll talk with the airline representative about *my* itinerary, explaining that I have important meetings in all these places, that my dates cannot be altered, and that I'll just have to work with another airline if a more reasonable airfare cannot be found."

When the next representative answered the phone, I lowered my voice, introduced myself as Mr. Sheppard, and then briskly listed the countries, continents, and dates that I needed to travel. The representative carefully listened to my itinerary, asked me a few questions, double-checked the dates I mentioned, and politely asked if she could put me on hold while she conferred with a colleague about the best possible airfare.

"Of course," I coolly responded.

After a few minutes, the representative came back on the line, polite as ever, and said, "Mr. Sheppard, just one more question, did your mother call earlier today?"

I froze, unable to speak for a long and awkward moment, quickly replaying in my mind our entire conversation and realizing how incredibly pretentious I had been.

"Um, yes," I finally said. "Mom sometimes helps me with these sorts of things."

"Ah, of course," the agent coolly responded, "that explains why my colleague priced out the exact same itinerary a short while ago. Your mother told us all about your big trip, Mr. Sheppard, and the airfare hasn't changed."

MOST PEOPLE DON'T REALIZE THE DISCIPLES OF JESUS MAY have been quite young. Contrary to medieval art and modern films that often portray the disciples as middle-aged men, it's much more likely they were somewhere between fifteen and twenty-five when they began following Jesus.

For example:

- From what we can tell, only Simon Peter appears to have been married. (Matt. 8:14–15 references his mother-in-law.) The typical age for a Jewish man to marry during this time was about eighteen years old, so you have to wonder if a number of the disciples were younger than that.
- Periodically, Jesus refers to his disciples as "little ones" (Matt. 11:25; Luke 10:21; John 13:33), which doesn't make much sense if they are middle-aged men.
- At one point, Jesus instructs Simon Peter to pay the Temple tax "for the two of us" (Matt. 17:24–27). According to Jewish law, you paid that tax only if you were over the age of twenty. The question is why didn't Jesus arrange to pay for the other disciples?[20]

This doesn't mean that *all* of the disciples were young (Matthew the tax collector, for example, already has a "real job"), but when you reimagine the stories of the disciples, picturing them as young people, it really does help to explain some things.

Like why, for example, the disciples are at times openly arguing with one another about who is the most important (Luke 9:46). Middle-aged adults, of course, might secretly wonder the same thing, but it's hard to imagine them openly arguing about their comparative greatness.

No, most of the disciples were younger than we think. And maybe that's why Matthew wants to be sure we know it was the Sons of Thunder—and their mom—who came to Jesus with such a bold and pretentious request.

If Jesus (like my friend and teacher Loren) believed in, spent time with, and wisely released young people into leadership, perhaps you and I should consider how we might do the same in our own areas of influence.

Ponder. Do you treat the young people in your life in a way that respects and encourages them in their abilities and potential?

Pray. Ask that you, like Jesus, will be able to see the God-given potential in others.

Practice. Make it a point to listen to, encourage, and consistently pray for someone who is younger than you—a friend, a sibling, your child, or a neighborhood kid.

CHAPTER NINETEEN

CONTAGIOUS TOUCH

*That's how Jesus came to be sitting at home with lots of
tax-collectors and sinners. They were there, plenty of them,
sitting with Jesus and his disciples; they had become his
followers.*

*When the legal experts from the Pharisees saw him
eating with tax-collectors and sinners, they said to his
disciples, "Why does he eat with tax-collectors and sinners?"*
—MARK 2:15

When my wife, Bronwyn, was about four years old, she was with her
mother at a shopping center, and they came across a serious looking
Sikh gentleman.

(The Sikh people, in case you don't know, are primarily from the
Punjab region of northern India and eastern Pakistan. Sikh men are
recognizable by their full beards and also by the fact that their long,
uncut hair is kept covered under a turban.)

Because Bronwyn had never seen a Sikh man before, and because
she had a children's picture-book Bible that portrayed the Pharisees
as dour individuals with turbans on their heads, Bronwyn naturally
assumed that this man in the shopping center must be a Pharisee.

So as she and her mom walked by this solemn Sikh gentleman,
in a loud and alarmed voice, Bronwyn yelled, "Look, Mommy, it's a
Pharisee!"

128

Thankfully, the kind gentleman had a good sense of humor. He laughed out loud at Bronwyn's comment and then responded to her embarrassed mother, "Well, at least she knows her Bible."

The problem, though, is that young Bronwyn did *not* know her Bible.

She knew that Jesus loved her—the most important thing of all—but four-year-old Bronwyn's view of scripture wasn't shaped (how could it be?) by a dynamic understanding of first-century history and all that it meant to be a Pharisee in that volatile, ancient setting.

So here's the critical question: Who were the Pharisees, really, and why were they so often butting heads with Jesus?

CONTRARY TO OUR MODERN IDEAS REGARDING PHARISEES and "their legalistic rules about how to get into heaven," first-century Pharisees were much more concerned with the here and now than they were with the hereafter.

The strict attention they paid to the Hebrew scriptures was not simply a personal obsession with not sinning. Rather, strict adherence to Torah was a political and social statement with significant cultural implications.

Not so unlike various groups today, Pharisees did not easily fit into a particular social, religious, or political box. To borrow an example from US politics, even if you are a registered Republican, you may well vote for a Democrat because of a particular issue (and vice versa).*

In that sense, the party is not the determining thing, the issue is.

And there were certain issues in the first century that were very important to the Pharisees, things like not working on the Sabbath day and not eating (or even associating) with certain people.

---

* I hasten to add that most Jewish people of this era were not card-carrying members of the Pharisees or of any other group in the first century, but they were, of course, interested in and influenced by the hot-topic issues of their age.

How you responded to these particular issues, in the mind of many Pharisees, determined whether you were in or out of the people of God. But Jesus, as he so often does, broke their boundaries. Because he redefined the rules of who was in and who was out solely around himself.

In a vintage and telling Jesus move, after he invites Matthew the tax collector to become his disciple (and tax collectors, mind you, were very much out in the mind of the Pharisees), Jesus makes it a point to take part in a big evening meal with plenty of riffraff in attendance:

> Later when Jesus was eating supper at Matthew's house with his close followers, a lot of disreputable characters came and joined them. When the Pharisees saw him keeping this kind of company, they had a fit, and lit into Jesus' followers. "What kind of example is this from your Teacher, acting cozy with crooks and riffraff?"
>
> Jesus, overhearing, shot back, "Who needs a doctor: the healthy or the sick? Go figure out what this Scripture means: 'I'm after mercy, not religion.' I'm here to invite outsiders, not coddle insiders." (Matt. 9:10–13 *The Message*)

For Jesus, sharing a meal with outsiders—acting cozy with crooks and riffraff—was one of the primary ways he was welcoming them in.

POPULAR THOUGHT IN JESUS' DAY ASSUMED THAT SIN WAS contagious. It was sin that made the people suffer. It was sin that kept Messiah from coming. According to some Pharisees, if there was any hope at all of deliverance from the oppression of Rome, it was because they had successfully protected themselves and their people from the viral and foreign contagion of sin.[21]

For Jesus, though, sin wasn't the most contagious thing in the world—he was.

Historian Marcus Borg captures this essential difference of perspective when he writes of the "contagious" holiness of Jesus.[22] You can witness this contagious effect at work in a moving story in the gospel of Luke:

> There was a woman who'd had an internal haemorrhage for twelve years. She had spent all she had on doctors, but had not been able to find a cure from anyone. She came up behind Jesus and touched the hem of his robe. Immediately her flow of blood dried up.
>
> "Who touched me?" asked Jesus.
>
> Everybody denied it. "Master," said Peter, "the crowds are crushing you and pressing you!"
>
> "Somebody touched me," said Jesus. "Power went out from me, and I knew it."
>
> When the woman saw that she couldn't remain hidden, she came up, trembling, and fell down in front of him. She told him, in front of everyone, why she had touched him, and how she had been healed instantly.
>
> "Daughter," said Jesus, "your faith has saved you. Go in peace." (8:43–48)

The reason the woman is trembling in this story, afraid to tell Jesus and the crowd about what she has done, is because her flow of blood, according to the traditional understanding of Torah in that day, meant that she was "unclean." Touching Jesus would have made him unclean too.

But here again, Jesus is redefining the boundaries of clean and unclean, of who is in and who is out, and he wants this woman, suffering and excluded for twelve long years, to know that she is in!

This story is made even more powerful by realizing that the hem or fringe of Jesus' robe that the woman touches were tassels that the Torah instructed every devout Jewish person to wear as an ever-present reminder of their unique and holy calling as the people of God.[23]

According to Jesus, and in radical contrast to the influence of many Pharisees, being holy wasn't just about avoiding the contagious effect of sin, and it most certainly wasn't about avoiding contact with a particular kind of people.

No, Jesus showed us that holiness is about how we treat others, especially those who are suffering and those who are different, those who may well be outsiders to your way of living, your way of voting, and, yes, your way of believing.

Ponder. Who are the outsiders in your community, at your school, or at your workplace, and have you ever shared a meal together?

Pray. Ask that you will know how to lovingly disagree with those who think differently than you do without demonizing them in the process.

Practice. Befriend someone who sees the world differently than you—someone from a different culture, someone who votes differently, someone who believes differently.

CHAPTER TWENTY

MARY, MARY

On their journey, Jesus came into a village. There was a woman there named Martha, who welcomed him. She had a sister named Mary, who sat at the master's feet and listened to his teaching.

—LUKE 10:38–39

Jesus' twelve disciples were all men, but they were not his only disciples. The gospel of Luke, in particular, makes this point clear in two passages.

The first comes in Luke 8:1–3, when the gospel writer explains that as Jesus was traveling through several villages and towns, ministering in each community, he and his twelve disciples were "accompanied by various women."

Luke goes on to identify the various women: "Mary, who was called Magdalene, from whom seven demons had gone out, Joanna the wife of Chouza (Herod's servant), and Susanna, and many others."

According to the gospel, not only were these women traveling with Jesus and the twelve disciples, which was already highly unusual, but apparently these women were also funding Jesus' day-to-day ministry through their own resources. Luke wants us to understand that Jesus' ministry, in its foundational stage, was uniquely dependent upon women.[24]

But Luke doesn't leave the issue there.

Just two chapters later, he introduces a pair of sisters, Martha and

Mary, who are hosting Jesus in their home. After explaining that Mary "sat at the master's feet and listened to his teaching," Luke continues with the story:

> Martha was frantic with all the work in the kitchen.
>
> "Master," she said, coming into where they were, "don't you care that my sister has left me to do the work all by myself? Tell her to give me a hand!"
>
> "Martha, Martha," he replied, "you are fretting and fussing about so many things. Only one thing matters. Mary has chosen the best part, and it's not going to be taken away from her." (Luke 10:38–42)

One of the most unusual parts of this story is how Martha speaks to Jesus. The tone she takes with him is nearly one of reprimand, isn't it? It's as if Martha is scolding Jesus for the way he is interacting with her sister.

Can you hear the resentment and exasperation in her voice? "Master," she said, "don't you *care*?"

Martha, we should understand, like all of the earliest friends and followers of Jesus, was on a journey of discovering who Jesus was. For better or for worse, that meant Jesus' friends were willing to be themselves with him.

In Martha's case, that meant being sassy.

Martha gets sassy with Jesus because Mary is defying a social norm by sitting at the master's feet—a privilege reserved in that culture for men only—and, incredibly, Jesus is just letting it happen.

IN THE FIRST CENTURY, TO SIT AT THE FEET OF A MASTER-teacher implied a teacher-student relationship. Luke uses this expression to describe Paul's apprenticeship with a famous Jewish teacher in Acts 22:3, when it says that Paul "studied at the feet of Gamaliel."

By describing Mary and Jesus this way, Luke wants his first-century audience to understand something significant: Mary has been welcomed by Jesus as a student, as a disciple, as an apprentice in his way of living.

"It is not difficult to imagine what is going through Martha's mind," explains Kenneth Bailey in his insightful study *Jesus through Middle Eastern Eyes*. "In all likelihood she is thinking: *This is disgraceful! What will happen to us! My sister has joined this band of men. What will the neighbors say? What will the family think? After this who will marry her? This is too much!*"[25]

"Martha, Martha," Jesus finally interrupts.

Don't miss the warm tone of his voice here, the steady repetition of her name, as if to say, "Martha, I hear you. Martha, I understand. But, Martha, you are wrong."

"You are fretting and fussing about so many things," Jesus says. "Only one thing matters. Mary has chosen the best part, and it's not going to be taken away from her."

Jesus will simply not allow Martha to keep her sister, Mary, confined to the kitchen.

THE MARY OF THIS STORY IS NOT THE ONLY MARY WHO followed Jesus. As it turns out, the name Mary appears fifty times in the gospel accounts alone. (It was a pretty popular name back then.) Eleven of those times refer to the Mary in our story, but fourteen of those references are about another Mary, the one who was "called Magdalene" (Luke 8:2).

Much has been made in recent years about Mary Magdalene's relationship with Jesus. Bestselling novelist Dan Brown, for example, came up with an intriguing, conspiratorial story about how Jesus and Mary Magdalene had a secret child together (which, by the way, no serious historian believes).

In reality, as is the case with our knowledge of most of Jesus' friends and followers, we know very little about Mary Magdalene. We know she was delivered of seven demons, we know she traveled with Jesus and his companions, we know she was there when he was crucified, and—most remarkable—we know she was the first person to see Jesus alive again after his death (Luke 8:1–3; Mark 15:40; John 20:11–18).

We will explore that resurrection appearance in part 5, but for now it's enough to say that the fact that Jesus chose this Mary as the first witness of his resurrection speaks volumes about the unique and important friendship they shared.

For their friendship to be special, for it to be unique, certainly does not mean we need to come up with a secret backstory about a hidden love affair. (Surely that's more of a commentary on our society than it is on Jesus and Mary Magdalene.)

But it does raise some important questions:

Did Jesus experience physical attraction to others?

Did he ever wonder what it would be like to be married?

Did he feel the absence of an everyday close companion?

The gospel records simply do not tell us about that part of Jesus' life, so all we can do is wonder.*

DOROTHY SAYERS (1893–1957) WAS A BRILLIANT WRITER, poet, and playwright, and, like the two Marys in our gospel accounts, she was a devoted follower of Jesus.

In a collection of essays that Sayers wrote about the role of women in society, she addressed the unique way Jesus interacted with women:

A prophet and teacher who never nagged at them, never flattered or coaxed or patronized . . . who rebuked without (demeaning) and praised without condescension; who took their questions and arguments seriously; who never mapped out their sphere for them,

---

* For what it's worth, I think Jesus did experience physical attraction to others (why wouldn't he?) and that others were attracted to him too (why shouldn't they have been?), but that being single was a spiritual discipline in his life because of his calling and vocation. So if you are single, let Jesus' single life encourage you, because he gets it.

never urged them to be feminine or jeered at them for being female; who had no axe to grind and no uneasy male dignity to defend.[26]

"Perhaps it is no wonder," she concludes, "that women were first at the Cradle and last at the Cross. They had never known a man like this Man—there has never been such another."

Ponder. The twelve disciples of Jesus were all men, which was the cultural norm for that time, but those twelve men were not the only disciples of Jesus.

Pray. Ask that you, like Jesus, will have healthy friendships with women and men alike.

Practice. In the books you read, the messages you listen to, and the counsel you receive, make it a point to learn from both women and men.

CHAPTER TWENTY-ONE

THE ROCK

"If it's really you, Master," said Peter in reply, "give me the word to come to you on the water."
"Come along, then," said Jesus.
Peter got out of the boat and walked on the water and came toward Jesus.

—MATTHEW 14:28–29

There's some real irony in Jesus' calling his friend Simon by the name Peter, because Peter means "Rock," and Simon Peter wasn't exactly the most stable of characters.

When you study Peter's life, one of the interesting things you'll note about his journey with Jesus is how often Peter is passionately communicating something only to be interrupted. For example:

- After Jesus explains to his disciples that he will be beaten and killed, the gospel of Matthew records that "Peter took [Jesus aside] and began to tell him off. 'That's the last thing God would want, Master!' he said. 'That's never, ever going to happen to you!'

    "Jesus turned on Peter. 'Get behind me, Satan!' he said. 'You're trying to trip me up! You're not looking at things like God does! You're looking at things like a mere mortal!'" (Matt. 16:22–23).
- Then, after Peter, James, and John witness Jesus transfigured

in light and observe him talking with the lawgiver Moses and the prophet Elijah, the gospel of Matthew records, "Peter just had to say something. 'Master,' he said to Jesus, 'it's wonderful to be here! If you want, I'll make three shelters here—one for you, one for Moses, and one for Elijah!'

"While he was still speaking, a bright cloud overshadowed them. There came a voice out of the cloud. 'This is my dear son,' said the voice, 'and I'm delighted with him. Pay attention to him'" (Matt. 17:4–5).

- Finally, a number of years after the resurrection, during a foundational and dynamic period of rapid growth in the early Jesus movement, the author of the book of Acts recounts the important story of Peter going to meet with a brand-new believer named Cornelius.

  According to the narrative, as Peter is preaching a message to Cornelius and to those who are gathered in his house, the Holy Spirit interrupts him midmessage: "While Peter was still speaking these words, the holy spirit fell on everyone who was listening . . ." (Acts 10:44).

If you've been following this chain of events, you will note that Peter has now been interrupted by Jesus, the Father, and the Holy Spirit—all three members of the Trinity!—quite an embarrassing accomplishment for the Rock.[27]

PETER WAS ONE OF JESUS' CLOSEST COMPANIONS. ACCORDING to the gospel accounts, Peter, James, and John spent more time with Jesus than anyone else, and of these three, Peter stands out most.

As to why Peter is given such prominence in Jesus' inner circle, there appear to be two practical reasons: Peter was most likely the oldest (remember, he was probably the only one married), and Peter was definitely the boldest.

I think it was probably the combination of these two things, Peter's age and his audacity, that resulted in his often leading the other disciples. The best known of these moments is when Peter boldly claims that Jesus is the King, the Messiah, to which Jesus wholeheartedly replies:

> "God's blessings on you, Simon, son of John!" answered Jesus. "Flesh and blood didn't reveal that to you; it was my father in heaven. And I've got something to tell you, too: you are Peter, the rock, and on this rock I will build my church . . ." (Matt. 16:17–18)

But it wasn't just this singular moment of courageous faith that made Peter stand out from the other disciples. Apparently, Peter was saying and doing these sorts of things on a regular basis.

Take for instance that mind-altering moment when the disciples see Jesus walking on the Sea of Galilee. At first they are convinced that it's a ghost, but after Jesus assures them that it's him, the gospel of Matthew goes on to say:

> "If it's really you, Master," said Peter in reply, "give me the word to come to you on the water."
>
> "Come along, then," said Jesus.
>
> Peter got out of the boat and walked on the water and came toward Jesus. (Matt. 14:28–29)

For years I read that story and thought, "Wow, Peter must have had such amazing faith to step out of the boat and onto the sea!"—which is certainly true. But it was in reading this story through the lens of Jesus' humanity that the down-to-earth nature of Peter's faith really began to make sense.

A NUMBER OF YEARS AGO WHILE I WAS TEACHING ABOUT the humanity of Jesus in Lausanne, Switzerland, at a YWAM Discipleship Training School, a bright young man named Jordan approached me after the session. For a few minutes we discussed a number of stories from the gospel, carefully unpacking each episode and exploring it through the lens of Jesus' humanity.

Somewhere along the way, the story of Jesus and Peter walking on the Sea of Galilee came up. I shared something simple about the relationship of a first-century rabbi and his disciple, and how that may have been part of what motivated Peter to ask if he could join Jesus on the water.

All of a sudden, Jordan went quiet. He was staring right at me, but at the same time he was looking beyond me, as if he was trying to figure out something before he asked me what was really on his mind.

"So," Jordan finally said, "are you saying that when Peter gets out of the boat and steps onto the water, he hasn't yet fully realized that Jesus is God?"

"Exactly!" I exclaimed. "That's probably why Peter had the courage to step out of the boat and on to the water in the first place," I continued, "because there was *another human* already out there."

JESUS' HUMANITY WAS A GIVEN FOR THE DISCIPLES, BUT HIS divinity was not. They could confirm his humanity because he stood right in front of them, but his divinity was a truth they grew into believing. Once we understand that, the gospel accounts come alive in a whole new way.

Undoubtedly, this astonishing moment of Jesus and Peter walking on the water is one of the moments that led the disciples to begin believing that Jesus was more than just Messiah (Matt. 14:33), but that does not mean the disciples suddenly had all their Jesus-and-God theology sorted out. (Do you?)

(Remember, just two chapters later, in Matthew 16:22, Peter takes Jesus aside to "tell him off," an action that does not make any historical sense if Peter is convinced by then that Jesus is somehow God.)

When Peter sees Jesus walking on the Sea of Galilee, I really doubt he's thinking to himself, "Oh, there's God, taking a stroll on the water."

It's much more likely that Peter is thinking something along the lines of, "If that's really Jesus, my master-teacher, then maybe he'll teach me to do that too."

Here's the takeaway for you and me: we don't know the exact point when the disciples became fully convinced that Jesus was somehow God, but what we do know is that they were always convinced that he was human.

Ponder. In your own journey with Jesus, do you need more convincing of his divinity or of his humanity?

Pray. Pray for the down-to-earth faith and audacity of Peter, who watched what his master, Jesus, did and then asked if he could join him.

Practice. Reread the stories of Jesus with this simple understanding in mind: Jesus' humanity was a given for the disciples, but his divinity is a truth they grew into believing. (By the way, this understanding also can transform your conversations about Jesus with your friends who are not yet convinced Jesus is God. Don't feel like you have to convince them. You can trust Holy Spirit to do that part.)

CHAPTER TWENTY-TWO

CONTAGIOUS KINGDOM

Jesus called together the Twelve, and gave them power and authority over all demons, and to cure diseases. He sent them out to announce God's kingdom and cure the sick.
—LUKE 9:1–2

After this the master commissioned seventy others, and sent them ahead of him in pairs to every town and place where he was intending to go.
—LUKE 10:1

The disciples of Jesus were his closest companions and most trusted friends. At times, they must have felt like they had a backstage pass to the most electrifying show on earth:

- They were there when Jesus preached his famous Sermon on the Mount.
- They were there when he multiplied fish and bread to feed five thousand.
- They were there when he healed the centurion's servant by saying the word.
- They were there when he was led from the garden to be scourged and crucified.
- They were there when he unveiled his death scars after being resurrected from the dead.

For three years the disciples saw and experienced it all, and, amazingly, they remained convinced that Jesus meant it when he said to them, "Come, follow me."

Let me explain.

The calling of a first-century disciple was to become like the disciple's master. When a master-teacher (or rabbi) invited you to follow them, it was much more than an invitation to sit, listen, and learn from them. It was an invitation to experience, absorb, and imitate them—to become like them.

"It involved a literal kind of following," write Ann Spangler and Lois Tverberg in *Sitting at the Feet of Rabbi Jesus*. "The task of the disciple was to become as much like the rabbi as possible."[28]

This probably explains why, at a strategic moment in Jesus' public ministry, he sends out his disciples to do exactly what he has been doing, which is announcing God's kingdom, casting out demons, and healing the sick.

WHEN IT COMES TO JESUS' MIRACLES, IT SEEMS MOST PEOPLE today fall into one of two camps. On the one hand, there is what I like to call the Superman group, and on the other, there is what I like to call the Thomas Jefferson group.

The Superman group believes that Jesus was and is something akin to an extraterrestrial superhero. "Yes, Jesus looks like a normal human being," this viewpoint says, "but he was born with special powers, enabling him to do special things, like heal people, walk on water, raise the dead."

(For what it's worth, many Christians fall into this Superman group, with the caveat that the reason Jesus was able to perform miracles was because he was God.)

In opposition to this perspective, many people are convinced the first-century stories were simply recorded in an exaggerated way. "Jesus was not at all like Superman," this viewpoint argues, "and he certainly didn't do any miracles, because that sort of thing doesn't happen."

One of the founding fathers of America, Thomas Jefferson, is a classic example of this second way of thinking, which is why Jefferson took a razor blade to the gospel records and removed all of the miraculous stories. (Seriously, he did.)

The earliest friends and followers of Jesus, though, were not bound by either of these viewpoints. When it comes to miracles, the portrait they paint of Jesus is that of a very real human being doing clearly miraculous things.

And most amazing of all is that Jesus—God in the flesh—invites his obviously human friends and disciples to join him in doing this miraculous work.

IT'S IMPORTANT TO NOTE THAT, ACCORDING TO THE GOSPEL accounts, Jesus begins to do miracles *after* he was baptized, *after* he felt the power of the Holy Spirit come "upon him" in the Jordan, *after* he heard the voice of the Father saying, "You are my son, my dear son!" (Luke 3:22).*

(Again, if Jesus was performing miracles earlier in life—like in his childhood—surely the gospel writers would mention it, but they don't.)

Why is this order of events important?

Because it teaches us two significant things about Jesus' journey and about the ministry he passes on to his disciples:

1. Jesus was rooted in the love of Abba before he began his public ministry.
2. Jesus was anointed by the Holy Spirit for power in ministry.

---

* I am in no way suggesting that Jesus *became* the Son at the moment of his baptism, which is a theological concept known as adoptionism. Rather, I am suggesting that Jesus was anointed in a unique way with power at his baptism, which is what the gospel writers seem to indicate.

Let's look at each of these significant points in turn.

First, throughout the whole of his ministry, Jesus never loses sight of the fact that first and foremost he is rooted in the love of the Father. "Everything," Jesus says in Luke 10:22, "has been given me by my father."

His identity in sonship (the secure, confident trust in the love and approval of Abba that we witness at his baptism) is what carries Jesus throughout his public ministry. More than anything else, according to Jesus, he is the Son of the Father, and that is what ultimately matters.

"Don't celebrate having spirits under your authority," Jesus tells his friends when they come back rejoicing because the demons are submitting to them. "Celebrate this, that your names are written in heaven" (Luke 10:20).

"Celebrate that Abba Father knows you," Jesus is saying, "that Abba Father loves you, and that Abba Father is for you."

Second, note the surprising way Peter describes Jesus when he is preaching about him in the book of Acts: "God anointed this man, Jesus of Nazareth, with the holy spirit and with power," Peter proclaims. "He went about doing good and healing all who were overpowered by the devil, since God was with him" (Acts 10:38).

This passage, we must understand, comes from an event that takes place years after the resurrection. You might think Peter would simply say, "Jesus did supernatural things because he was God," but Peter doesn't quite do that. Instead, he locates the source of Jesus' power in the anointing of the Holy Spirit.

That raises all sorts of interesting questions:

- Did Jesus—again, God in the flesh—limit himself in his humanity so that he was reliant upon the Holy Spirit's anointing for miracles?
- Did this powerful anointing for miracles come after Jesus' baptism, after the Holy Spirit came "upon him" in the Jordan?
- Did Jesus intentionally operate in this way—reliant upon

the Holy Spirit's anointing—because he wanted to teach his disciples to do the same?

Only God knows the answers to these questions, of course, and we must hold our opinions lightly. But what we can be confident of is that Jesus intends for his kingdom to spread. It is a contagious kingdom.[29] The presence and power of the Holy Spirit is now available to us all. Jesus' radical invitation, "Come, follow me," still stands.

Because of Jesus' humanity—his life, death, and resurrection—there is now a new way to be human: deeply rooted in the love of Abba Father and overflowing with the life and power of the Holy Spirit.

Ponder. Jesus was deeply rooted in the love of Abba Father before he began his public ministry, and he was anointed with the Holy Spirit's power for his ministry. Are you?

Pray. Ask for the love of Abba Father to be deeply rooted in your heart as you do what you are called to do today. (Let the words of Romans 8:14–17 help you as you pray.)

Practice. Make it a point, at various moments in your day—perhaps morning, noon, and night—to simply remind yourself, "More than anything else, I am a child of God."

CHAPTER TWENTY-THREE

BUT WAS HE FUNNY?

News of him at once reached a woman who had a young daughter with an unclean spirit. She came and threw herself down at his feet. She was Greek, a Syrophoenician by race; and she asked him to cast the demon out of her daughter.

"Let the children eat what they want first," Jesus replied. "It's not right to take children's bread and throw it to the dogs."

"Well, Master," she said, "even the dogs under the table eat the crumbs that the children drop."

"Well said!" replied Jesus. "Off you go; the demon has left your daughter."

So she went home, and found the child lying on the bed and the demon gone.

—MARK 7:25–30

When it comes to understanding this story, it seems to me we have only two options.

Option one: Jesus responds to this woman in a rude and racially demeaning way, but then, thankfully, he has a sudden (and somewhat inexplicable) change of heart and decides to heal the woman's daughter after all.

Option two: there is something in the look of Jesus' eyes, in the tone of his voice, in the expression on his face that enables this woman to realize she is being asked a riddle of sorts, and she nails the answer.

From everything we know of Jesus, the second option is really the only option. Clearly, Jesus is joking with this woman.

(I imagine Jesus with a grin on his face in this story, on the verge of laughter all the way through, nodding his head in proud approval of the woman's quick wit, and finally giving his bewildered disciples a look of "Isn't she wonderful!")

"Hold on a second," someone might say. "Yes, Jesus was kind, and I know he was compassionate and powerful—but, seriously, was he funny?"

WHILE THERE ARE ALL SORTS OF ADJECTIVES ONE MIGHT use to describe the way Jesus communicated, the word boring is certainly not one of them.

Jesus loved to tell a good story, particularly when it had a surprising punch line. He was all about the use of hyperbole and irony, and he occasionally employed a little sarcasm too. Jesus was a genius at using unforgettable imagery to convey punchy and powerful messages, and apparently he thought camels were especially funny, because he used them often in his imagery.

Let's look at each of these points in turn.

Good Stories and Surprise Endings. Just think about the memorable characters and scenes that Jesus introduced in his parables. There's the good Samaritan, the generous landowner, the unjust judge, the noisy neighbor, the sower and the seeds, and so many more. Jesus enjoyed telling a compelling tale, and maybe never more so than when the ending caught people off guard.

Take the parable of the prodigal, for example (Luke 15:11–32). When the parable begins, you think the story is all about the youngest son wildly and recklessly spending the family fortune. By the end of the tale, you realize the story is primarily about the father wildly (and recklessly, according to the elder brother) spending a fortune to celebrate his lost son's return home.

Jesus loved that kind of surprise ending.

Hyperbole, Irony, and a Touch of Sarcasm. "The kingdom of heaven," Jesus said, "is like a grain of mustard seed . . . It's the smallest of all the seeds, but when it grows it turns into the biggest of the shrubs. It becomes a tree, and the birds in the sky can then come and nest in its branches" (Matt. 13:31–32).

Now, a few of those details may not be technically true: the mustard seed is not the smallest of seeds, it does not become the biggest of shrubs, and it does not necessarily then become a tree. No, Jesus is using hyperbole to make a point.

Jesus enjoys the use of humorous irony too. "Follow me," Jesus famously said to Simon and Andrew, "and I'll have you fishing for people!" (Mark 1:17). Obviously, you don't go fishing for people (you go fishing for fish), but saying such a thing to blue-collar fishermen, writes Elton Trueblood in his interesting and insightful book *The Humor of Christ*, most likely would have elicited a smile from Simon and Andrew before they left their nets and followed him.[30]

Thankfully, when it comes to sarcasm, Jesus uses this particular form of ironic jest sparingly, because sarcasm can be quite cutting. A classic example is when Jesus confronts the religious hypocrisy of the Pharisees. "Well, good for you," Jesus tells them at one point. "You get rid of God's command so you won't be inconvenienced in following the religious fashions!" (Mark 7:9 *The Message*).

Yep, that burn had to hurt.

Unforgettable Imagery to Convey a Message. "How can you say to your neighbor, 'Here—let me get that splinter out of your eye,'" Jesus asked, "when you've got the plank in your own?" (Matt. 7:4). Plain and simple, Jesus is making a joke here (drawing on his background in carpentry, no less), and people probably would have laughed out loud when he said it.

But they would have laughed even harder when Jesus turned his quick wit on the Pharisees with this cultural zinger: "You're blind guides! You filter out a gnat, but you gulp down a camel!" (Matt. 23:24). Picture it: the overly-religious Pharisees are carefully straining every sip of water to make sure they don't swallow a miniscule gnat, but they've never noticed the massive hairy hump of a camel swishing around in their mouths.

Regardless of your cultural background, that's a pretty funny picture, but one of the reasons Jesus and his first-century Jewish audience would have found the gnat-and-camel imagery really funny is because it's also a witty wordplay in Aramaic: "You filter out a *galma*," Jesus says, "but you gulp down a *gamla!*"

That's just genius: brilliant wordplay, unforgettable imagery, and impeccable delivery all wrapped up in one hilarious comeback.

Having heard Jesus relentlessly mock the Pharisees this way, people would have walked away that day laughing with one another, talking about Jesus' sharp wit, and going home to tell their friends and family, "Did you hear the one about the Pharisee straining a *galma* and swallowing a *gamla!*"

I USED TO BE AFRAID OF BEING FUNNY WHENEVER I TALKED about religious things because I was under the impression that comedy is somehow less spiritual than other forms of communication. But that was before I really explored the life of Jesus.

Think about it: Was Jesus any more holy when he was fiercely and angrily flipping over tables in the Temple (Luke 19:45) than when he was grinning at the Syrophoenician woman and asking her a riddle before he heals her daughter?

No, of course not. Jesus was just being Jesus.

He knew when to be serious.

He knew when to be compassionate.

And, thank God, Jesus knew when to laugh.

I think one of the reasons we never really hear much about the humor, hilarity, and joy of Jesus is because so many people (perhaps

Christians most of all, God forgive us!) are genuinely and tragically convinced that God is far too serious to ever have a good time.

Jesus, however, begs to differ, and I think that Syrophoenician woman—witty, wise, and desperate—recognized the mischievous spark in his eyes right from the start.

Ponder. "Seriousness is not a fruit of the Spirit, but joy is" (Garreth Gilkeson, preacher and percussionist, commenting on Galatians 5:22–23).[31]

Pray. Ask for more joy, jubilation, and genuine laugh-out-loud moments in your life.

Practice. As best you can today, depending on your circumstances, make it a point to take yourself a little less seriously: breathe deeply, smile unreservedly, and trust wholeheartedly.

CHAPTER TWENTY-FOUR

HUMAN THOUGHTS

As the time came nearer for Jesus to be taken up, he settled
it in his mind to go to Jerusalem. He sent messengers
ahead of him. They came into a Samaritan village to get
them ready, and they refused to receive him . . . When the
disciples James and John saw it, they said, "Master, do
you want us to call down fire from heaven and burn them
up?" He turned and rebuked them, and they went on to
another village.

—LUKE 9:51–56

The Sons of Thunder really were something, weren't they? Before Jesus rebukes them here, I can't help but wonder if he's thinking, "Really, since when did you two learn how to call down fire from heaven?"

In the gospel of Luke, this story takes place shortly after Jesus entrusts his disciples with the authority to announce God's kingdom, cast out demons, and heal the sick. "So off they went . . ." the narrative reads, "announcing the good news and healing people everywhere" (Luke 9:6).

Apparently, at least in James and John's case, this new endowment of power rapidly goes to their heads, and these two brothers now imagine themselves like the prophet Elijah in the Hebrew scriptures, able to call down fire from heaven to demonstrate their authority (1 Kings 18).

Jesus immediately (and from what we can tell, strongly) puts the

153

Sons of Thunder in their rightful place: "He turned and rebuked them . . ." (Luke 9:55).

The gospel doesn't provide any details of the rebuke, but I think we can imagine it:

First, picture the other disciples, some of them probably agreeing with the fiery zeal of James and John, but others perhaps giving one another that knowing look of "Uh-oh, Jesus is *not* going to like this idea. Somebody's definitely about to feel the heat, but it's not going to be the Samaritans."

Then imagine Jesus stopping in the middle of the road, turning to face James and John, and just staring at them. At first, maybe the boys are thinking, "The Sons of Thunder are about to add a little lightning to our repertoire," but then it dawns on them that the fiery look in Jesus' eyes is directed not toward the village but toward them.

Finally, picture James and John standing there after receiving a stinging rebuke from their master, sheepishly looking at one another, and then both of them saying to Jesus at the same time, "It was *his* idea."

WHEN JESUS GETS UPSET, HE CAN BE PRETTY FIERCE. THE gospel of Mark records an event when Jesus encounters a man with a withered hand on the Sabbath day, a day on which the religious leaders claimed that any kind of work whatsoever, even health care, should not be done.

Jesus asks the leaders:

"Is it lawful to do good on the sabbath, or to do evil? To save or to kill?" They stayed quiet.

He was *deeply upset* at their hard-heartedness, and looked around at them *angrily*. Then he said to the man, "Stretch out your hand." He stretched it out—and his hand was restored. (Mark 3:4–5, italics added)

A similar scenario plays out in the gospel of Luke when on a Sabbath day Jesus heals a woman who is bent double with crippling arthritis. Once again, the religious leaders object to the Sabbath day healing and Jesus angrily responds:

> "You bunch of hypocrites!" replied Jesus. "You would all be quite happy to untie an ox or a donkey from its stall on the sabbath day and lead it out for a drink! And isn't it right that this *daughter of Abraham*, tied up by the satan for these eighteen years, should be untied from her chains on the sabbath day?" (Luke 13:15–16, italics added)*

Each of these stories, while standouts in their own right, fade in comparison with the startling moment when Jesus lashes out at Peter and compares him to the devil after Peter scolds Jesus for explaining to the disciples he will be killed.

Peter is convinced, along with everyone else, that the role of Messiah cannot possibly include suffering and dying, so he takes Jesus aside to try to talk some sense into him. "Get behind me, Accuser!" Jesus forcefully responds to his friend Peter. "You're thinking human thoughts, not God's thoughts" (Mark 8:33).

But what exactly are the human thoughts that Jesus is resisting with such force, going so far as to compare one of his best friends to the devil?

WHEN I WAS ABOUT EIGHTEEN YEARS OLD, THE HOLY SPIRIT asked me a question in my heart: "Do you want to know God or do you want to be known by people?"

---

* By the way, while it was common for Jewish men in this time to be called *sons of Abraham*, there are only three examples in ancient Hebrew literature of the phrase *daughter of Abraham* being used, and it is always in reference to Israel as a whole. Here, however, for the first time in recorded Hebrew history, Jesus uses this groundbreaking identity marker—daughter of Abraham—in reference to one Jewish woman. Jesus is not just healing this woman's body, he is also affirming this woman's dignity and acknowledging her unique identity.

I wish I could tell you that I once and for all answered that question then and there, settling the matter in my heart for good. Unfortunately, though, it's a question I have had to answer again and again, because there is a dangerous part of me that sometimes longs for glory, honor, and the approval of others more than I long to know and love God.

The problem is that my answer to that question is at times a multilayered yes.

We don't know much about the origin of the devil, but the Bible seems to suggest that he was at one time a glorious archangel of sorts, but pride—pure and evil pride—led to his downfall (Isa. 14:12–15; Ezek. 28:12–19).

Apparently, the devil's desire to be known (to have it his way, on his terms, according to his claims) vanquished his desire to know God.

The abiding problem with sin is that each and every one of us now is tempted with that same cancerous desire. We want life our way, on our terms, according to our claims, because we think we know better than God. It is the idolatry of self.

I think these are the human thoughts to which Jesus is responding with such force in this story:

The human thoughts that led Adam and Eve to take and taste sin in the first place.

The human thoughts that led the Hebrew people to turn away to other gods.

The human thoughts that whispered to Jesus in the wilderness, "There's another way to be Messiah—just take it."

But Jesus refuses to take the bait, refuses to function from human thoughts alone, refuses to operate the way that the disciples and everyone else are expecting the Messiah to operate: by establishing the rule and reign of God through a violent military campaign. "No!" Jesus is saying. "That is not at all how the kingdom of God works."

After he forcefully puts Peter in his place (not so unlike what he had to do with James and John), Jesus tells his disciples of another way to live:

"If any of you want to come the way I'm going," he said, "you must say no to your own selves, pick up your cross, and follow me. Yes: if you want to save your life, you'll lose it; but if you lose your life because of me and the message you'll save it. After all, what use is it to win the world and lose your life?" (Mark 8:34–36)

Ponder. The idolatry of self (in all its forms: arrogance, self-centeredness, visions of personal grandeur, self-pity, forcing your will on others) is a cancerous evil that must be confessed and fought.

Pray. Ask that a desire to know and love God will overwhelm and displace the human thoughts that lead us away from living, loving, and trusting like Jesus.

Practice. In my own journey with Jesus, there is no better way to resist the idolatry of self than by (1) looking up to God in worship, and (2) looking out to others in service.

PART FOUR

BLOOD, SWEAT, AND TEARS

*"My father," he said, "if it's possible—please,
please let this cup go away from me! But . . .
not what I want, but what you want."*
—MATTHEW 26:39

CHAPTER TWENTY-FIVE

HOLY FURY

They came into Jerusalem. Jesus went into the Temple and
began to drive out the traders, those who bought and sold
in the Temple, and overturned the tables of the money-
changers and the seats of the dove-sellers . . .
 "Isn't this what's written," he said,

> *'My house shall be called*
> *A house of prayer*
> *For all the world to share'?*

 "But you've made it a brigand's den!"
 —MARK 11:15–18

It's what Jesus did and said in the Temple that finally led to his execution. Each of the gospel writers, in their own way, makes this point clear (Matt. 21:46; Mark 11:18; Luke 19:47; John 11:48).

But what did Jesus do and say in the Temple that was so dangerous?

To answer that question, we need to understand a few critical points in Jesus' journey that led to this moment:

- Shortly before the Temple showdown, according to the gospel of Mark, Jesus begins to teach his disciples "something new" (Mark 8:31). We will explore that something new in the next chapter, but the short version is this: according to Jesus, the

Messiah will be rejected, he will be killed, and after three days, he will be raised. Again, this is a radical departure from everyone else's expectation, which is why the Sons of Thunder in Luke 9:54, for example, assume that anyone who resisted Jesus would be consumed by fire, because that was the sort of Messiah they expected.

- Jesus arrives in Jerusalem just before the Festival of Passover, the most significant and sacred festival of the Jewish people. The holy city would have been heaving at this point, its population swollen by as much as ten times. In the middle of all that fanfare, Jesus enters Jerusalem with a large following of people who are claiming that he's the Messiah, the King who will deliver them from the power of Rome (Matt. 21:1–11).
- With people now shouting in the streets that Jesus is "David's son," the "coming one," the Messiah who will set them free (Matt. 21:9; Ps. 118:25–26), Jesus enters the Temple, which is the seat of power in Jerusalem, he observes all that is taking place there, and then, in a fit of holy fury, Jesus cleans house.

AS FAR AS I KNOW, I HAVE WITNESSED TRUE RIGHTEOUS rage only one time in my life. It was during my early teenage years, and my family and I were traveling.

We were in Paris, it was late at night, and we were carrying our luggage through an eerily empty subway corridor, trying to find our way to the place where we were staying. (This was before the advent of luggage with wheels, and I have a distinct memory of balancing my bags on top of my skateboard, which I carried with me everywhere at the time.)

Rounding a corner, we were surprised to hear a man angrily shouting at someone. I saw Dad give my older brother, Tré, a quick look, and then both of them picked up their pace. I followed.

As our family rounded the next bend, with my father and brother in the lead, we were stunned to witness a tall, broad-shouldered man hovering over a young woman who was shielding herself on the ground. The man was wearing a flamboyant purple three-piece suit, and he was yelling all sorts of obscenities, kicking and hitting the terrified woman at his feet.

He was her pimp and she was his prostitute.

The young woman, in a sequined miniskirt, was shaking with tears, and mascara was running down her face. She was desperately trying to fight back, but the man was just too powerful.

Even though the man was much larger than my father, Dad never hesitated, not even for a split second. He yelled at the top of his lungs, grabbed two of the biggest bags we had, and began sprinting toward the man with both bags swinging. Tré was right behind him (and so was I, skateboard in hand like a battering ram).

When he saw us coming, the man let the young woman go, directing his attention toward us instead. Free of his powerful grip, the woman raced for an exit, running up a nearby flight of stairs.

The man turned and threatened us as he backed away, warning us not to follow him and motioning he had a weapon. At that point, Dad stopped running and he made sure that we did too.

This was long before cell phones, so all we could do was stand there in the empty subway corridor and watch the man in the purple suit disappear up onto a dark side street. My father was shaking with righteous rage.

WHEN JESUS ENTERS THE TEMPLE IN JERUSALEM, HE'S NOT just upset, he's furious. "Zeal for your house . . . has consumed me," the psalmist says. "The insults of those who insult you have fallen on me" (Ps. 69:9; see also John 2:17).

Like this psalm of old, when Jesus observes what is happening in the Temple, he takes it personally, as if the offense against Abba Father is an offense against him.

The gospel writers describe three significant things that take place in rapid succession:

- First, Jesus flips over the tables of money changers and the seats of the dove sellers. One of the reasons he is so upset is because the chief priests and Temple leaders are making a handy profit from the vast numbers of pilgrims who are flooding Jerusalem for Passover. At very high rates, most likely, the people would have been forced to change their money into Temple coinage before buying an animal for sacrifice, and doves, in particular, were the affordable sacrifice if a family was poor.
- Second, when Jesus challenges the Temple system in this way (with the money system in disarray, no animals could be bought for the time being), he intentionally provokes the wrath of the Temple leaders. The chief priests and religious leaders publicly confront him and Jesus launches into a brilliant and blistering series of counter-confrontations, riddles, and parables that basically all say the same thing: the heart of the problem here is you! (Matt. 21:23–23:39).
- Finally, it's not only the corruption of the Temple system and its leaders that Jesus confronts with such fury, it's what the Temple itself has come to symbolize. What is supposed to be "a house of prayer for all the world to share" has instead become the white-hot symbol of the people's revolutionary fever to overthrow Rome—"a brigand's den!" Because of this radical reversal of God's intentions, Jesus proclaims the Temple itself will now be judged.[32]

The gospel of Mark wraps up this adrenaline-charged Temple episode with Jesus telling his disciples, "You see these enormous buildings? There will not be one single stone left on top of another. They will all be torn down" (Mark 13:2).

It's challenging to put into perspective just how radical a statement like that would be in first-century Jerusalem. For an imperfect but modern comparison, consider the impact of a substantiated rumor spreading, just days before a presidential election in the United States, that a leading candidate for the presidency had said to their inner circle, "The White House is coming down."

You had better believe that powerful figures on both sides of the aisle would conspire together about how best to deal with that candidate, and in a similar (but even more significant) way it caused an electrifying stir in first-century Jerusalem when rumors spread that Jesus—someone being called King—was talking about the Temple coming down.

The Temple, we must understand, "was the largest structure in the Roman world," and its surrounding area was the size of thirty-five football fields.[33] It was the center of the world for most Jewish people at that time, the holy space where heaven and earth met, the sacred heart of religious, cultural, and national life. To speak of its destruction was to speak of unthinkable judgment—a judgment, mind you, that the Temple leaders would have perceived as an indictment against their leadership.

From their perspective, that kind of Temple talk would never do. The leaders determined that something must be done about Jesus.

Ponder. There are some things worth getting angry about—particularly flagrant abuse of power and religious leaders' misrepresenting the heart of God—and Jesus understands that anger.

Pray. Ask that in your anger, you do not sin (Eph. 4:26).

Practice. Before you confront injustice, make sure the injustice is not at work in you.

CHAPTER TWENTY-SIX

HOLY WASTE

While Jesus was at Bethany, in the house of Simon (known
as "the Leper"), a woman came to him who had an
alabaster vase of extremely valuable ointment. She poured
it on his head as he was reclining at the table.
   When the disciples saw it, they were furious.
   "What's the point of all this waste?" they said. "This
could have been sold for a fortune, and the money could
have been given to the poor!"
               —MATTHEW 26:6–9

The story of the woman and the alabaster vase takes place shortly
after the epic showdown in the Temple. Because of all that has tran-
spired in the last few days, the disciples are on edge.

They're exhausted.

Imagine the emotional impact of being with Jesus as he entered
the city to the wild acclamation of the Passover crowds. "When they
came into Jerusalem," the gospel of Matthew says, "the whole city
was gripped with excitement" (21:10). Hundreds, if not thousands, of
people are caught up in the euphoric expectation surrounding Jesus at
this point—the wildfire hope that Jesus is the coming King who will
deliver his people from Rome's oppression—and the disciples are in
the center of it all.

They're confused.

While on the one hand the disciples are elated that Jesus finally seems to be embracing the people's expectation and desire for him to lead, at the same time, more than ever, Jesus is speaking in multilayered parables and stories that indicate he will be killed and that overwhelming sorrow and suffering is on its way to Jerusalem (Matt. 21:33–46).

They're afraid.

"Is he trying to bring it on himself?" the disciples must be wondering. "Doesn't he realize the leaders are plotting against him?" Undoubtedly, the disciples are also trying to process the stark implications of Jesus' stern warning about the Temple, that not a "single stone" will be left standing, that the entire Temple compound (keep in mind its vast size) will be coming down.

In the middle of all this, during a window of rare respite at an evening meal, a woman approaches Jesus with the alabaster vase. Silently, she breaks the precious seal and a costly fragrance fills the air.

Tenderly, reverently, she pours the valuable ointment on Jesus' head as if she is anointing him King.

That's when the disciples snap.

"What's the point of all this waste?" they said. "This could have been sold for a fortune, and the money could have been given to the poor!" (Matt. 26:8–9).

If he's not going to be King, what's the point?

If he's not going to lead the people, what's the point?

If he's not going to help the poor, the oppressed, the displaced, then what's the point?

"In God's name, Jesus," the disciples must be thinking by now, "if you're just going to be killed like every other wannabe Messiah, what's the point of all this holy waste?"

IN HIS LIFE AND MINISTRY, AND, VERY SOON, IN HIS DEATH, Jesus radically redefines the role of Messiah.

Yes, Jesus cares for the practical needs of the poor, the oppressed, and the displaced.

Yes, he will confront the systemic issues of evil that define their daily existence.

Yes, he intends to lead the people, to be the King they so desperately desire.

But, no, he will do none of those things in the way they want him to.

He will come not as military conqueror but as suffering servant.

If the ultimate solution to his people's pain and sorrow was as straightforward as providing more food, then surely Jesus would have just kept on multiplying fish and bread (Mark 6:30–44).

But Jesus is convinced the human predicament requires a much more radical remedy, a much more invasive surgery, to deal with the cancerous evil entrenched in the human heart since Eden.

Adam and Eve's way of being human must die.

It cannot simply be reformed or refashioned.

The serpent's lie and its deadly venom must be fully absorbed, drained, "exhausted" of its power.[34] The calling and vocation of Messiah is to draw the full measure of evil and its consequence onto himself and to trust God alone for vindication.

Yes, Jesus views the arrogance of Rome as an affront to the sovereignty of God.

Yes, Jesus longs for his people, and all people, to be free of sin's oppression.

Yes, Jesus believes his calling is once and for all to vanquish that foe.

But, no, Jesus will not attain that victory in the world's ways.

Instead, Jesus will do what Adam and Eve, Israel and her people, and indeed all people have failed to do: the Messiah will bear evil's full-force assault, but he will never draw from the devil's arsenal in his response.

He will turn the other cheek (Matt. 5:39).

He will love his enemies to the very end (Matt. 5:44).

He will cry, "Father, forgive them!" even as they crucify him (Luke 23:34).[35]

AS TO HOW JESUS CAME TO THIS NEW AND RADICAL UNDER-standing of Messiah, an understanding that results in his willing death at the hands of the Romans instead of his violently crushing the Romans, everything points to the Hebrew scriptures as his source.

With Abba Father and the Holy Spirit as his guide, Jesus weaves paradoxical passages from the prophets Isaiah, Daniel, Zechariah, and others to clarify details of his mysterious destiny. Jesus also draws from the psalms, one of which is the source of his cry from the cross—"My God, my God, why have you forsaken me?" (Ps. 22:1)—a psalm of profound faith and unyielding trust that we will explore in a later chapter.

In Jesus' eyes, we must understand, his death at the hand of sinners will by no means be a holy waste but will instead become his coronation as King. Jesus will be crowned, but it will be with a crown of thorns.[36]

Understandably, the disciples are terribly confused, even distraught, by the way Jesus is speaking about his impending death, which is why they respond so sharply to the woman with the alabaster vase.

"Jesus knew what they were thinking," the gospel account continues:

> "Why make life difficult for the woman?" he said. "It's a lovely thing, what she's done for me. You always have the poor with you, don't you? But you won't always have me. When she poured this ointment on my body, you see, she did it to prepare me for my burial. I'm telling you the truth: wherever this gospel is announced in all the world, what she has just done will be told, and people will remember her." (Matt. 26:10–13)

The next verse in the gospel of Matthew reads, "*Then* one of the Twelve, called Judas Iscariot, went to the chief priests. 'What will you give me,' he said, 'to hand him over to you?'" (26:14–15, italics added).

While all of the disciples are confused by what Jesus is saying and doing, the response of Judas Iscariot is different. He can no longer abide this mysterious talk of a crucified king, of an obscure and vague victory that somehow comes through death, because for Judas, Jesus has become a means to an end.

It's a deadly deception, and one that is common to us all: when our dreams and desires to see the kingdom come (i.e., change the world) eclipse and displace our love for and trust in the King.

Ponder. Does your desire to change the world (help the poor, save lost souls, care for the planet) at times eclipse and even displace your love for and trust in King Jesus?

Pray. Ask for your heart to be tender toward Jesus, like the woman with the alabaster vase.

Practice. In my own journey with Jesus, I've found there is no substitute for prayer and worship. Without it, King Jesus very subtly can become a means to an end in my life and work.

CHAPTER TWENTY-SEVEN

JESUS AND JUDAS

Jesus knew that the father had given everything into his hands, and that he had come from God and was going to God. So he got up from the supper-table, took off his clothes, and wrapped a towel around himself. Then he poured water into a bowl and began to wash the disciples' feet, and to wipe them with the towel he was wrapped in.
—JOHN 13:3–5

One betrays him, another denies him, and all of the disciples desert him, but a few hours before all that happened, Jesus does two significant things: he washes his disciples' feet and he serves them an awe-inspiring final meal.

While the gospel writers are not clear in their chronology as to whether Judas was still at the table when Jesus broke the bread and served the wine of Communion, the gospel of John makes it plain that Judas was present when Jesus washed the feet of his disciples.

"'And you are clean,'" Jesus says in the gospel of John, after he has washed the disciples' feet, "'but not all of you.' Jesus knew, you see, who was going to betray him. That's why he said, 'You are not all clean'" (John 13:10–11).

It's an arresting image: Jesus kneeling before Judas, washing the feet of the man, the disciple, the friend who will betray him.

Equally arresting is the fact that, according to Jesus, in the next few

171

hours each and every one of the disciples, even Simon Peter, the Rock, will be tested in ways that they cannot possibly imagine:

> "Simon, Simon, listen to this. The satan demanded to have you. He wanted to shake you into bits like wheat. But I prayed for you; I prayed that you wouldn't run out of faith. And, when you turn back, you must give strength to your brothers."
>
> "Master," replied Simon, "I'm ready to go with you to prison—or to death!"
>
> "Let me tell you, Peter," replied Jesus, "the cock won't crow today before you have three times denied that you know me." (Luke 22:31–34)

Note the poignant and painful switch of names in Jesus' conversation with Simon Peter. Jesus begins by calling him Simon, but after he protests that he will never deny him, it's as if Jesus says, "No, Rock, even you are about to break."

THE GOSPEL OF MATTHEW, DESCRIBING JESUS' FINAL HOURS, records that in the end "all the disciples abandoned him and ran away" (Matt. 26:56).

For the most part, we don't know where they went and what they did when they ran away, but the gospel of Matthew does provide descriptions of the actions of Simon Peter and Judas Iscariot.

In fact, Matthew records the actions of Peter and Judas one after the other, as if he wants the reader to see how these two different disciples responded.

(By the way, in the next two chapters, we'll return to various aspects of Jesus' final Passover meal with his disciples and his desperate praying in the garden of Gethsemane, but for now it is important to see Judas's betrayal and Peter's denial in light of Jesus' humility in washing their feet.)

The gospel of Matthew explains that after Jesus is apprehended by the authorities and taken to the high priest and elders to be tried, Peter "followed him at some distance . . . to see how things would work out" (26:58).

The story is well known:

- Peter hides himself among the servants in the courtyard of the high priest.
- One of the servant girls recognizes him as a companion of Jesus.
- Peter responds, "I don't know what you're talking about."
- Another servant recognizes him as well.
- Again, Peter denies it, swearing, "I don't know the man!"
- A number of the servants now join in: "You really are one of them!"
- Finally, in anger, Peter curses and swears, "I don't know the man!"

"And then, all at once, the cock crowed," Matthew writes. "Peter remembered . . . He went outside and cried like a baby" (26:74–75).

Only three verses after this description of Peter's weeping outside the courtyard, the gospel of Matthew continues Jesus' story by saying, "Meanwhile Judas, who had betrayed him, saw that he had been condemned, and was filled with remorse" (27:3).

Again, the story is well known:

- Judas rushes to the chief priests and elders, holding the blood money in his hands.
- "I've sinned!" he cries. "I betrayed an innocent man . . ."
- "See if we care!" they respond. "Deal with it yourself."
- Judas throws the money at their feet.
- Overcome with remorse, he races to a nearby field.
- In condemnation, regret, fear, and confusion, he ties the rope.
- Judas the betrayer, so recently with Jesus, now desperately alone, hangs himself.

JESUS WASHED THE FEET OF BOTH PETER AND JUDAS, BUT their lives, and indeed their deaths, could not have turned out more differently.

According to tradition, Simon Peter gave his life as a martyr in the early years of the Jesus movement. Judas Iscariot, however, committed suicide, never knowing of the history-altering, death-defeating event that came after Jesus' crucifixion.

Our knee-jerk reaction may be, "Good, I'm glad Judas hanged himself! After all, didn't Jesus call him the son of destruction in John 17:12?" (That verse, of course, can be interpreted in all sorts of ways.)

You can't help but wonder, though, what Jesus' postresurrection reaction to Judas might have been, especially taking into account the way Jesus responded to the rest of his disciples after his resurrection:

He forgave them.

He restored them.

He empowered them.

We will never know what might have happened because Judas, just like he did by betraying Jesus in the first place, took matters into his own hands.

What we do know is that, according to the book of Acts, the rest of the disciples did not gloat or take delight in Judas's death. If anything, there is a trace of profound sadness when Peter says of the betrayer, "He was counted along with us, and he had his own share in the work we've been given" (Acts 1:17).

Perhaps Peter is remembering that Jesus washed Judas's feet the same way he washed the feet of all the disciples, and that it just as easily could have been any of them, even Peter, who betrayed him.

Regret is a powerful, paralyzing, even life-threatening force, but it wasn't regret that killed Judas.

Because, remember, all of the disciples—not just Judas and not least Peter—had deep regrets about the final hours of Jesus' life.

No, in the end, it was Judas who killed Judas, because he had to have it his way.

Ponder. You can't help but wonder what the postresurrection Jesus might have said to his disciple Judas.

Pray. Pray for someone you know who is paralyzed by condemnation, regret, fear, and confusion, and if that's your experience, ask someone you trust to pray with you.

Practice. Choose to forgive someone who has hurt you, who has wronged you, who has perhaps even betrayed you, because Jesus has forgiven you.

CHAPTER TWENTY-EIGHT

EATING THE STORY

When the time came, Jesus sat down at table, and the apostles with him.
  "I have been so much looking forward to eating this Passover with you before I have to suffer," he said to them. "For—let me tell you—I won't eat it again until it's fulfilled in the kingdom of God."
  —LUKE 22:14–16

Humans are unique in that not only do we eat food to sustain us, but we also eat food to celebrate, to remember, to make moments meaningful. Celebratory mealtimes, in that sense, are a distinctly human phenomenon.

(That's why you've never witnessed, for example, a group of neighborhood cats placing birthday candles on a fish cake before singing in unison, or, for that matter, a devoted family of aardvarks solemnly bowing their heads to pray before digging into a delicious anthill.)

Meals don't just nourish humans. They mark us, they remind us, and sometimes, they even provide meaning for us.

One of the most meaningful meals I've ever experienced took place in England during my first year of marriage to Bronwyn. Together with a small team, Bronwyn and I were helping to lead a six-week summer event called Forty Days for one hundred college students and young adults. Our goal that summer was to make our way through the entire narrative of scripture through teaching, discussion, prayer, and action.

We wanted people to experience the Bible, to participate in the unfolding drama of it all, to somehow even enter the narrative itself.

My friend Nathan Johnson, a composer and creative genius, had a brilliant idea, something he'd been mulling over for years. "What if we were to communicate the entire arc of scripture through an elaborate meal," he suggested, "utilizing all five senses along the way, so that people are not simply listening to the story, but they are seeing, touching, hearing, smelling, and eating the story."

After a flurry of late-night meetings and long hours of preparation (not least by a gifted woman named Kristen, the chef among us), Nathan and our team served up the narrative-feast to the entire gathering.

We called it Quintessential. Twelve dishes made up the meal, with accompanying scents, songs, and visuals complementing each course. (Not to give too much of it away, but there were even crisp, red apples injected with vinegar, a bitter reminder of Adam and Eve's first taste of sin.)

Truly, it was a feast of biblical proportions, a sensory experience of the story of God that those of us who were there will never forget.

FOR THE JEWISH PEOPLE OF JESUS' DAY, THE FEAST OF Passover was a defining event. It was celebrated each and every year, family by family, in a particular way, with particular food.

This annual feast was a reminder of how God delivered the Hebrew people from slavery in a foreign land: while their slave drivers were judged, they were passed over, delivered, set free. With that specific event in mind, each time they celebrated the Feast of Passover, it was as if they were eating the story of freedom.

While we don't know all the details of a first-century Passover meal, we can be fairly confident that at the very least it included these four essential elements: family, food, wine, and song.

- The family would have gathered in a common area, most likely around a table that was low to the ground. Each person would have been seated on the floor, leaning on pillows or reclining against a family member or friend. (In the ancient world, there was symbolism in this way of sitting, as "only free people had the luxury of reclining while eating.")[37] After a customary blessing and a meandering retelling of the Hebrew people's earliest history, it was the honored task of a child to ask the traditional question, "Why is this night different from all other nights?"

- The food, in so many ways, was the deep and meaningful answer to that question. Again, we don't know for sure what all of the various parts of a first-century Passover meal might have been, but it's likely that bread and lamb and bitter herbs, among other things, would have been present. The bread was flat, prepared without any leaven, a reminder of the people's rapid exodus from Egypt when they were slaves. The lamb was a symbol of sacrifice, a sacrifice that caused death to pass over them. The herbs were bitter, a sign of their suffering as slaves.

- The wine flowed freely at different points during the feast, and there may have been as many as four cups, each a sign of an aspect of their freedom or deliverance. For example, they were (1) freed "from slavery," (2) delivered by God's "mighty acts," (3) liberated to be God's "people," and (4) released to "the land" God promised to their ancestors (Ex. 6:6–8). Each cup of wine, rich and red, would have tasted of deliverance, and in that sense, it was a drink of life, a toast to liberation, a cup of freedom.

- The songs came at various points in the meal. As a benediction of sorts, a number of the psalms would have been sung (Psalms 115–118), songs that reminded the people of their salvation in days past, songs that looked forward to their coming Messiah. Because even though the Passover feast urged the people to look back and recall their deliverance from slavery long ago, it also urged them to look forward to the day when they would finally be set free from all oppression—in this case, even the oppression of Rome.

WITH THAT CRASH COURSE IN HEBREW HISTORY IN MIND, and remembering that this particular feast was a meal that Jesus and the disciples would have celebrated every year since they were children, consider the impact of what Jesus does at a Passover meal shortly before he is crucified.

Someone, maybe the youngest of the disciples, would have already asked the time-honored question: Why is this night different from all other nights?

Jesus responds:

> While they were eating, he took bread, blessed it, broke it, and gave it to them.
>
> "Take it," he said. "This is my body."
>
> Then he took the cup, gave thanks, and gave it to them, and they all drank from it.
>
> "This is my blood of the covenant," he said, "which is poured out for many." (Mark 14:22–24)

It's almost impossible for us to hear the weight of those words the way the earliest friends and followers of Jesus did. Because it's as if he is saying:

> The story you have been eating all these years,
> the story that stretches back to Passover,
> the story that reaches forward to freedom,
> that story is standing before you here and now,
> talking and breathing and heart-beating,
> in my body, in my blood,
> in my humanity.

Incredibly, and mindblowingly for those who were present that night, Jesus is telling his friends that the entire narrative of scripture, the whole arc of history, has led to what he is about to accomplish on the cross.

Because of Jesus' humanity, because of his body and his blood, eating the story will never ever be the same.

So the next time you participate in Holy Communion, when the bread touches your teeth and you drink deeply of God's profound goodness from the cup, may you encounter again the breathing, heart-beating, flesh-and-blood humanity of King Jesus.

Ponder. For Jesus' earliest friends and followers, those who were there that Passover night, bread and wine would never taste the same.

Pray. Ask that the overwhelming wonder of Holy Communion, the Eucharist, the Lord's Supper, will enable you to truly "taste and see that the LORD is good" (Ps. 34:8).

Practice. The next time you receive the bread and wine, whisper this simple reminder to yourself before you eat and drink: "Why is this meal different from all other meals?"

CHAPTER TWENTY-NINE

ANOTHER GARDEN

They came to a place called Gethsemane.
—MARK 14:32

There are two great gardens in history: Eden and Gethsemane. (Actually, there are three, but that's getting ahead of our story.)

In the first garden, as recounted in the book of Genesis, humanity made the life-and-death choice to listen to the lie of the serpent, to abandon the love of Creator, to go against God's design for humans.

In the second garden, as seen and experienced in the life of Jesus, humanity is again faced with a life-and-death choice, but this time, with this human, in this garden, the decision is different.

Shortly after Jesus serves his disciples the bread and wine of communion, he leads them to a nearby olive grove to pray (the name Gethsemane comes from the Aramaic, which literally means "olive press"):

"Stay here," said Jesus to the disciples, "while I pray."

He took Peter, James and John with him, and became quite overcome and deeply distressed.

"My soul is disturbed within me," he said, "right to the point of death. Stay here and keep watch." (Mark 14:32–34)

Jesus' vulnerability in this moment is striking. He knows he is coming into a time of intense testing and overwhelming suffering, and he wants his three closest friends near.

181

Yes, Jesus wants them to keep watch (because his captors are now on their way), but I also imagine that Jesus doesn't want to be alone. The desperate language Jesus uses with his friends when he speaks of his soul being "disturbed within . . . to the point of death" is akin to someone crying, "The tension is killing me!"

It's as if Jesus is somehow wrestling with life and death in his prayers. According to the gospel of Luke, Jesus is praying in such "agony" of soul that "his sweat became like clots of blood, falling on the ground" (22:44).

THIS IS NOT CREATIVE LICENSE OR HYPERBOLE FROM LUKE, who was a doctor.* The medical term for the rare occurrence of sweating blood is hematohidrosis. It can happen when overwhelming emotional, physical, and mental stress causes the little blood vessels surrounding our sweat glands to burst open and bleed.

While it's impossible for us to understand and to identify with all that is going on in Jesus' mind and heart at this moment—and thank God we will never have to—what the garden of Gethsemane does reveal is Jesus' incredible capacity to identify with us.

For example:

Have you ever been afraid of physical harm?

Jesus knows what that feels like.

Have you ever been afraid of death and what follows?

Jesus knows what that feels like.

Have you ever been afraid the path in front of you is far too difficult?

Jesus knows what that feels like.

Have you ever been afraid that God will not rescue you in the way you desire?

I think Jesus knows what that feels like.

"He must have known that he might have been deeply mistaken . . .,"

---

* Doctor Luke was a traveling companion of the apostle Paul, and Paul refers to Luke's medical background in Colossians 4:14.

explains N. T. Wright in *Jesus and the Victory of God*. "It was, after all, a huge gamble. Messiahs were supposed to defeat the pagans, not to die at their hands."[38]

If Jesus did not have real fears and questions about what was in front of him, about his crucifixion and what would follow, then his pleading prayers in Gethsemane make little sense. We must not make this wrestling in prayer into a moment of divine playacting for Jesus.

There are gnawing questions about his identity and destiny, his suffering and death at work here. There are whispering lies of the enemy tempting and taunting him from every side, urging Jesus in another direction.

Questions and concerns, stress and fear—all of these are terrifyingly real for Jesus in Gethsemane, which is one of the reasons why those little capillaries surrounding Jesus' sweat glands burst open and bleed.

Remarkably, through it all, in the face of every fear, temptation, and lie, Jesus refuses to abandon his trust in Abba Father:

> He went a little further, and fell on the ground and prayed that, if possible, the moment might pass from him.
>
> "Abba, Father," he said, "all things are possible for you! Take this cup away from me! But—not what I want, but what you want."
> (Mark 14:35–36)

JESUS CHOOSES TO ENDURE THE CROSS BECAUSE HE TRUSTS the Father, because he believes, in the words of the book of Hebrews, that there is "joy spread out and waiting for him" on the other side of his suffering and death (12:2).

In the midst of the blood, sweat, and tears of Gethsemane, what Jesus has been telling his disciples all along—that the Messiah must suffer, must be killed, must be raised again to new life—the excruciating extent of that calling is hammered out (think *proekopten*) in the agonizing place of prayer.

There is no other way for the evil of sin and its consequences to be undone:

Jesus will vanquish the power of evil by absorbing all its power,
he will represent humanity in the court of all accusers,
he will substitute himself in place of his people,
he will ransom his life in exchange for ours:
and in the end, Jesus trusts, he will be vindicated as King,
   by the power of God.

Even though Jesus trusts Abba, it does not remove or lessen the terrifying reality of what he will soon experience on the cross. One can hear his sense of agony in the sharp tone he uses with his disciples when he finds them sleeping in Gethsemane instead of watching and praying. "You can sleep now," Jesus says, "and have a good rest! Look—the time has come . . ." (Matt. 26:45).

According to Matthew, while Jesus is still speaking, Judas arrives with a large band of soldiers, sent from the chief priests and elders to arrest him. "My friend," Jesus says to his disciple Judas, "what have you come to do?" (26:50).

Thankfully, we will never experience the agony that Jesus endured in Gethsemane, but because of what he endured in that garden, each and every one of us can be assured—in our most tormenting moments of fear—that Jesus understands.

Ponder. In Gethsemane, Jesus chooses to endure the cross because he trusts Abba, because he believes God will rescue him in the end (Heb. 12:2).

Pray. Ask that in your moment of deepest sorrow, you will remember Jesus: "He put up with enormous opposition from sinners. Weigh up in your minds just how severe it was; then you won't find yourselves getting weary and worn out" (Heb. 12:3).

Practice. Remind yourself, over and over if needed, and especially in those moments when you feel desperately alone and like you are about to break: Jesus understands.

CHAPTER THIRTY

SHARING THE BURDEN

*Then the high priest got up in front of them all and
interrogated Jesus . . .*
    "Are you the Messiah, the Son of the Blessed One?"
    *"I am," replied Jesus, "and you will see 'the son of man
sitting at the right hand of Power, and coming with the
clouds of heaven.'"*
    *"Why do we need any more evidence?" shouted the
high priest, tearing his clothes. "You heard the blasphemy!
What's your verdict?"*
    They all agreed on their judgment: he deserved to die.
        —MARK 14:60–64

Because of the things Jesus was saying and doing, those in authority had
to do something about him. They could either follow Jesus as King or
denounce him as dangerous. In the end, the forces of religion and politics
conspired, as they so often do, and decided to make an example of him.

The radical actions of Jesus in the Temple and his open confrontation with its leadership meant that the emerging movement surrounding
Jesus was now seen as something of a counter-Temple movement. "If
we let him go on like this," the chief priests and leading elders said,
"everyone is going to believe in him! Then the Romans will come and
take away our holy place [Temple], and our nation!" (John 11:48).

Once Jesus is betrayed and put on trial (and after accusations are leveled against him because of rumors of what he has said about the Temple), the high priest pointedly asks him, Are you claiming to be King of the Jews? ("the Messiah, the Son of the Blessed One"; Mark 14:61). Up until this point in the trial, Jesus has been silent. Now he responds—"I am"—and quotes a significant prophecy from the Hebrew scriptures (v. 62).

Jesus' words come from the book of Daniel: "I saw one like a human being [the literal translation is 'son of man'] coming with the clouds of heaven. And he came to the Ancient One and was presented before him. To him was given dominion and glory and kingship, that all peoples, nations, and languages should serve him. His dominion is an everlasting dominion that shall not pass away, and his kingship is one that shall never be destroyed" (7:13–14).

That title, Son of Man, and how Jesus uses it in reference to himself is what leads to the charge of blasphemy from the high priest. To put it simply, not only does Jesus claim to be the Messiah, or King, but as King he also claims to be the Son of Man, a mysterious, heavenly, human-divine-like figure in Hebrew prophecy who somehow shares the authority and glory of the "Ancient One"—God.[39]

Because of this "blasphemous" claim, the chief priests and elders condemn Jesus to die.

WITH A DEATH SENTENCE PENDING, JESUS IS TAKEN TO Pilate, the Roman governor. Even though the Temple leaders exercised significant governing oversight, they were not entrusted with the legal authority from Rome to put anyone to death. For Jesus to be executed, he would have to be condemned by Pilate as well:

> "We found this fellow," they said, "deceiving our nation! He was forbidding people to give tribute to Caesar, and saying that he is the Messiah—a king!"
>
> So Pilate asked Jesus, "You are the king of Jews?" (Luke 23:2–3)

Because various first-century sources reveal Pilate to be a vindictive and power-hungry leader who was particularly antagonistic toward Jewish people, I believe Pilate's question here is cutting and flippant and should by no means be understood as a serious inquiry as to Jesus' identity. (I emphasize this point because of a long and tragic tradition of "Christian" anti-Semitism that has sought to make Pilate look like a blameless Roman accomplice in the crucifixion.)

The gospel of Mark records that after a great deal of back-and-forth on both sides, and finally because of Pilate's political pandering and the chief priest's insistence, Pilate "had Jesus flogged, and handed him over to be crucified" (15:15). He was to be executed as a rebel against Rome, as an enemy of the state, with the charge against him that he claimed to be "King of the Jews" (Mark 15:26).

The practice of flogging or scourging a revolutionary-criminal before crucifixion was standard Roman practice at the time and was particularly brutal:

- The victim was stripped of their clothes and their hands tied upright to a wooden post or an iron stake in the ground.
- The instrument of abuse was a sturdy handheld whip made of multiple leather strands, intertwined with weighted pieces of iron, rock, and bone.
- The aim was to sink the hard fragments into the victim's back, torso, and legs, and then pull up, down, or sideways, producing deep lacerations.

After Jesus was severely beaten and formally scourged in this way, the gospel of Mark records that the Roman soldiers dressed him in purple, placed a crown of thorns on his head, and then mock saluted him as the King of the Jews:

"Then they led him off to crucify him. They compelled a man called Simon to carry Jesus's cross. He was from Cyrene, and was coming in from out of town. He was the father of Alexander and Rufus" (Mark 15:20–21).

CHAPTER THIRTY-ONE

NO ESCAPE

When they came to the place called Golgatha, which means
Skull Place, they gave him a drink of wine with bitter herbs.
When he tasted it, he refused to drink it.

—MATTHEW 27:33–34

The book of Proverbs offers straightforward advice for someone who is dying: "Give strong drink to one who is perishing, and wine to those in bitter distress; let them drink . . . and remember their misery no more" (Prov. 31:6–7).

If ever there was a time when Jesus needed relief from pain, a pain so dire that it exceeds human understanding, surely the cross was it.

He's been up all night, sweating blood in the garden.

He's been mocked, beaten, and scourged by a regiment of soldiers.

He's suffering tremendous blood loss, so much so that he cannot carry his cross.

Once Jesus arrives at Golgatha, and just moments before the Roman soldiers drive eight-inch iron nails through his flesh, tendons, and bone, he is offered a pain reliever, a drink to temporarily dull his senses, a sedative that will make it easier for the soldiers to hammer their way into his broken body.

But Jesus refuses the drink.

He refuses to dull his mind, his will, his emotions.

He refuses to escape the present, painful, agonizing reality of his life. Why?

THE DESIRE TO ESCAPE LIFE'S CIRCUMSTANCES, PARTICU-
larly its challenges, is a deeply human experience, a predicament that
each and every one of us can identify with and relate to in one way or
another.

It's why our favorite television show is so appealing at the end of
a long day.

It's why that bottle of beer, that glass of wine, that mixed drink
tastes so good.

It's why we wrestle with end-of-life choices, whether to "let someone go."

When it comes to the complicated subject of escape, though, there
are no easy answers or one-size-fits-all solutions:

For one person, that television show or movie is a simple and
refreshing way to relax, to provoke, to be inspired. For another, it's a
desperate, fleeting attempt to cope, to soothe, to seek an alternate story
to their painful reality.

For one person, that bottle of beer or glass of wine is a gift-of-the-
earth way to celebrate the end of a day, the end of a week, the special
holiday. For another, it's a chain 'round their neck, a numbing device
they don't know how to live without.

For one person, the hard decision not to resuscitate, not to revive,
not to hold on to a suffering loved one is heartbreakingly merciful.
For another, it's a convenience, a decision made of selfishness, not
sacrifice.

God alone can see the inner workings of our hearts and minds, of
why we do the things we do (and we must not judge ourselves or others
too harshly), but when Jesus refuses the drink offered him, I believe it
is because of one reason:

Jesus refuses the sedative because he is refusing to accept any unintended consequences of his deep desire to escape what he is experiencing.

Of course Jesus wants to ease his pain!

Of course Jesus wants to dull his sorrow!

Of course Jesus wants to escape his agony!

But he will not risk—no, he *must* not risk!—the clarity of his mind, the strength of his will, and the control of his emotions in this most significant and final trial of his life and calling as Messiah. For King Jesus, there can be no escape.

IN THE HOUR OF HIS GREATEST SUFFERING, THE BEAUTY of Jesus' life is resplendent. A lifetime of prayer, of walking close with Abba, of making the hard choices, of "beating" his way forward against the tempting pull of broken humanity; all of the fruit of what it means to be filled with the Spirit—to be "Christlike"—in the purest and truest sense of the phrase; all of that and more is now seen in Jesus.

He doesn't snap.

He doesn't panic.

He doesn't give up.

No, when Jesus hears women weeping and mourning on his behalf, distraught at what he is suffering, he seeks to care for them instead (Luke 23:27–31).

When the soldiers drive the iron stakes through his wrists and into his ankles, he cries, "Father, forgive them! They don't know what they're doing!" (Luke 23:34).

When one of the criminals crucified beside him speaks of a distant day when, somehow, Jesus will "become king," he tells that criminal that today is that day and "you'll be with me . . ." (Luke 23:42–43).

And, finally, in a scene so moving that it's almost too beautiful to believe, too sacred to witness, the gospel of John tells us that before Jesus breathes his final breath, when the weight of the world is on his shoulders, he makes sure that his mother, weeping there at the foot of the cross, is taken care of by one of his disciples. Mary must not be left alone. "*After* this," the gospel of John says, "Jesus knew that *everything* had at last been completed" (19:28, italics added).

IF IT IS TRUE THAT WE HAVE SEEN THE FACE OF GOD IN JESUS,
then never was that face more beautiful than in the glory and passion
of his suffering on the cross:

> I am not moved to love you, Lord,
> By promises of paradise;
> Nor does the hell that terrifies
> Move me to want to sin no more.
>
> You are the one that moves me, Lord,
> When to your cross I turn my eyes
> To see your wounds, hear insults, lies;
> I'm grieved to know you're dying, Lord.
>
> Your love moves me in such a way
> That without heav'n I'd love you still,
> And without hell, I'd fear to stray.
>
> I need no goads or giveaway;
> For even if my hopes were nil,
> I'd love you as I do today.

The author of this old Spanish poem, "Sonnet to Christ Crucified,"
is unknown, but the poet has captured the tone, the feel, the reverent
and astonished wonder of the gospel accounts of Jesus' suffering so well.

When it comes to the crucifixion, instead of starting with what
Jesus' death means for you or with an abstract theory of atonement, the
writers of the gospel first want us to see, to experience, to encounter
the mystery and majesty of Jesus on the cross, and to know that this,
more than anything else, is what God looks like.

Once that earth-shifting truth gets into us, that the clearest portrait
of God we will ever see is of Jesus—the one who suffered in our place
on the cross—everything else will soon follow.

In so many ways, we are that criminal beside Jesus, condemned to die as all humans are, the cancer of sin and its consequences coursing through our veins like a terminal blood disease. But then, unexpectedly and overwhelmingly, we discover another suffering beside us, another suffering our fate, another dying our death. It is undeserved, unmerited, and breathtakingly beautiful, and all we can do in the presence of such glory is whisper in amazement, "King Jesus."

Ponder. "You are the one that moves me, Lord / When to your cross I turn my eyes / To see your wounds, hear insults, lies / I'm grieved to know you're dying, Lord."

Pray. Ask for a deeper, truer, more visceral understanding of Jesus' crucifixion, not just an intellectual understanding of a theory of atonement but an experience and encounter with the one who was crucified.

Practice. Consider your mechanisms of escape and their unintended consequences: What changes do you need to make?

CHAPTER THIRTY-TWO

IN THE END

At midday there was darkness over all the land until three in the afternoon. At three o'clock Jesus shouted in a powerful voice, "Eloi, Eloi, lema sabachthani?" Which means, "My God, my God, why did you abandon me?"
—MARK 15:33–34

Then Jesus shouted at the top of his voice, "Here's my spirit, Father! You can take care of it now!" And with that he died.
—LUKE 23:46

Jesus was nailed to the cross at about nine in the morning, and he died between three and six that same day. During those hours of excruciating sorrow (the word crucifixion, by the way, is where we get our word excruciating from), Jesus uttered at least seven different words or sayings from the cross:

- "Father, forgive them! They don't know what they're doing!"
- "I'm telling you the truth, you'll be with me in paradise, this very day."
- "Mother, look! There's your son. Look! There's your mother."
- "My God, my God, why did you abandon me?"

- "I'm thirsty."
- "It's all done!"
- "Here's my spirit, Father! You can take care of it now!"*

There is a lifetime of meaning in Jesus' final words from the cross, both in what they meant to him and also in what they mean for you, for me, and for humanity.

"Good Friday," wrote the late Father Richard John Neuhaus in his discerning book *Death on a Friday Afternoon*, "forms the spiritual architecture of Christian existence. And the Seven Last Words embody the truth of Good Friday."[40]

There is scandalous grace (not once, but twice!), tender affection, dark desperation, agonizing thirst, long-and-hard-fought-for accomplishment, and in the end, before Jesus finally lets go of his unbreakable spirit, there is the simple, unyielding trust of a child.

ACCORDING TO THE GOSPEL ACCOUNTS, AND LUKE IN PARTI-cular, Jesus' final words from the cross are bookended by his relationship with Abba Father. His passion on the cross begins with his crying, "Father, forgive them! They don't know what they're doing!" and his passion ends with the words, "Here's my spirit, Father! You can take care of it now!" still on his lips (Luke 23:34–46).

In between these two statements is the dark, distant, and mysterious, "My God, my God, why did you abandon me?" (Mark 15:34).

In Mark's telling of the event, the gospel writer wants to make sure we know that Jesus utters those words "in a powerful voice." In other words, "This is not a confused, bitter, resigned whimper of surrender," the gospel of Mark is saying. "No, Jesus said those words with force, in a powerful voice, as if he wanted the whole world to hear."

---

* These words or sayings of Jesus from the cross are listed in traditional order: Luke 23:34, Luke 23:43, John 19:26–27, Mark 15:34/Matthew 27:46, John 19:28, and Luke 23:46.

While it's impossible to know all that is taking place in Jesus' mind in this central moment of his suffering, what we can know is that the words "My God, my God, why did you abandon me?" are not randomly selected. These words, desperate and severe, are by no means arbitrary. Jesus is quoting Psalm 22.

Jesus quotes only the first line (which was the typical way of referring to a psalm in this time), but it only makes sense, particularly in view of how this specific psalm unfolds, that Jesus would have had the entire psalm in mind:

> My God, my God, why have you forsaken me?
>> Why are you so far from helping me . . .?
> I am a worm, and not human;
>> scorned by others, and despised by the people. . . .
> I am poured out like water,
>> and all my bones are out of joint . . .
>> you lay me in the dust of death.
> For dogs are all around me;
>> a company of evildoers encircles me.
>> —PSALM 22:1–16

The psalm, however, thanks be to God, does not stop there, not by a long shot:

> But you, O LORD, do not be far away!
>> O my help, come quickly . . .
> For he did not despise or abhor
>> the affliction of the afflicted;
> *he did not hide his face from me.* . . .
> All the ends of the earth shall remember
>> and turn to the LORD;
> and all the families of the nations
>> shall worship before him . . .

and proclaim his deliverance to a people yet unborn,
saying that he has done it.
—PSALM 22:19–31, ITALICS ADDED

It is vital for us to have the whole of this psalm in mind when we hear Jesus quoting these loaded and significant words from the cross, "My God, my God, why did you abandon me?" If not, we may commit the serious mistake of suggesting (and, God forbid, sometimes even insisting) that the Father in a legalistic, transactional way abandoned his Son in this moment to somehow appease divine wrath toward sin—and any sort of legal requirement to appease divine wrath is something that Jesus never ever suggests of his Father.

Having experienced the full-force assault of evil and all of its consequences on the cross—and from that abysmal, lonely, desperate place of sin-wracked, fallen humanity that still cries, "My God, my God, why did you abandon me?"—Jesus, our representative and our substitute, places his trust, his life, his death, and his spirit in the never-forsaking care of Abba Father:

"Then Jesus shouted out at the top of his voice, 'Here's my spirit, Father! You can take care of it now!' And with that he died" (Luke 23:46).

I WILL NEVER FORGET WHEN BRONWYN AND I FIRST TOLD our two oldest children, Miréa and Blaze, about Jesus' death.

They were still quite young, and we were somewhat apprehensive about telling them, but we wanted to be sure they heard the story from us, and not from a well-meaning but deeply misguided Sunday school teacher who might tell them Jesus was punished by God for all the bad things they had done.

So after a number of months of telling Miréa and Blaze stories about Jesus from the gospel accounts—about the man who healed blind people and who opened deaf ears, about the man who told such amazing stories of how much God loves us, about the man who multiplied fish and bread and walked on water, about the man who taught his friend to walk on water too, about the man who everyone was hoping would one day become King—at long last, once they learned to like and to love this man, we told them the story of how Jesus died.

We offered them no theological theories of the crucifixion in that holy moment.

We just told our kids the story, as best we knew how.

And both of them were very, very quiet.

It was our eldest, Miréa, who at last broke the silence. She was crying, and so were we.

"Daddy," she said, "will God help Jesus? Will God give him his life back?"

I looked to Bronwyn, not sure what to say or do, but we had already determined together that we would let the story linger for the night, without resolution.

"It's late," I finally whispered in response, "and we need to sleep. But tomorrow morning, I promise you, Daddy and Mommy will tell you the rest of the story."

Ponder. Jesus' final words from the cross are bookended by his trust-filled relationship with the Father, and the rest of his words should be read through that understanding.

Pray. Ask for the faith, hope, and love of a child.

Practice. When introducing the crucifixion of Jesus to others, particularly children, let the story speak for itself first, instead of imposing a particular theological view on top of it. Remember, the point is not to introduce someone to a theological viewpoint or to a theory of atonement. Rather, the point is to introduce someone to a person, Jesus.

PART FIVE

BREAKFAST ON THE BEACH

When they came to land, they saw a charcoal fire
laid there, with fish and bread on it . . .
"Come and have breakfast," said Jesus to them.
—JOHN 21:9–12

CHAPTER THIRTY-THREE

SILENT SATURDAY

Now there was a man named Joseph . . . from Arimathea,
a town in Judaea, and he was longing for God's kingdom.
He approached Pilate and asked for Jesus's body. He took it
down, wrapped it in a shroud, and put it in a tomb hollowed
out of the rock, where no one had ever been laid. It was the
day of Preparation, and the sabbath was beginning.
    The women who had followed Jesus, the ones who
had come with him from Galilee, saw the tomb and
how the body was laid. Then they went back to prepare
spices and ointments. On the sabbath they rested, as the
commandment specified.
    —LUKE 23:50–56

The gospel of Luke reveals next to nothing about the day after Jesus died, other than "they rested, as the commandment specified."

After the mad, adrenaline-laced tragedy of the last twenty-four hours, culminating in their long-hoped-for king being brutally executed on a Roman cross, the friends and followers of Jesus were undoubtedly exhausted. Spent in body, wearied in mind, their emotional well-being strained to the point of breaking, the rhythm and rest of Sabbath would have arrived as a gift.

But I doubt that any of them rested well on that sacred Sabbath day, because when Jesus was crucified, their hopes and dreams died with him.

203

er failed Messiah.

other failed revolution.

Another failed attempt to change the world.

"Be kind to me, GOD," the psalmist cries in chapter thirty-one, "I'm in deep, deep trouble again. I've cried my eyes out; I feel hollow inside. My life leaks away, groan by groan . . ." (31:9–10 *The Message*).

Sometimes sorrow runs so deep we have no words to pray. That is when the book of Psalms comes to our rescue, because the psalms, uniquely, honestly, even exquisitely, pray for us and through us.

I feel confident that on Silent Saturday, the day after Jesus died, his friends and followers would have sought solace in the psalms. That's what Jewish people do. They may even have found particular comfort in Psalm 31, because it was from this psalm that Jesus uttered his dying prayer: "Into your hand I commit my spirit . . ." (31:5).

Only a few verses earlier, the psalmist prays, "In you, O LORD, I seek refuge; do not let me ever be put to shame . . . rescue me speedily" (31:1–2).

"If only God had rescued Jesus," his friends and disciples must have been thinking on that dreadfully still, quiet, in-between day. "If only God had intervened."

THERE IS AN ANCIENT HOMILY THAT CAN BE READ ON Silent Saturday. "Something strange is happening," the haunting words begin,

> There is a great silence on the earth today,
> a great silence and stillness.
> The whole earth keeps silence because the King is asleep . . .[41]

Please don't misunderstand the word asleep here. By no means is this suggesting that Jesus was not really dead inside that dark, empty tomb where Joseph of Arimethea and the others laid him.

When the Roman soldiers crucified Jesus, they knew what they were doing—these were professional executioners after all. According to the gospel of John, the soldiers even plunged a spear into his side to be absolutely sure he was dead, "and blood and water came out" (19:34).

Make no mistake, John is saying Jesus was dead. The life within him, that mysterious spark or breath of existence we call spirit or soul, was gone.

But the question is this: Where exactly did Jesus' life go?

The scriptures, I'm afraid, do not clearly provide an answer.

On the one hand, you have Jesus saying to the bandit on the cross beside him, "I'm telling you the truth, you'll be with me in *paradise* this very day" (Luke 23:43, italics added). On the other hand, you have Peter's earliest letter claiming that, "In the spirit, too, [Jesus] went and made proclamation to the spirits in *prison* . . ." (1 Peter 3:19, italics added).

And then there's that curious passage in the book of Acts which speaks of the Messiah "not being left in *Hades*," which is a reference to something King David said in Psalm 16:10 (Acts 2:31, italics added). Finally, add to all that the early Christian conviction, as vividly expressed in the Apostles' Creed, that, somehow, Jesus "descended into hell."[42]

Paradise, prison, Hades, hell . . .

The only thing clear is that after Jesus breathes his last, entrusting his spirit to the Father, there are deep and cosmic mysteries at work in the heart of eternity itself—mysteries, mind you, that I doubt we will ever fully understand.

And that is where poetry and art, the mysterious stuff of which that ancient homily is made, are so helpful in attempting to articulate what was taking place on Silent Saturday when the body of Jesus was lying breathless in a tomb.

"God has died in the flesh," the homily continues, "and hell trembles with fear,"

> ᴜ gone to search for our first parent, as for a lost sheep.
> ᴜreatly desiring to visit those who live in darkness and the
>   shadow of death,
>   he has gone to free from sorrow the captives Adam and Eve . . .[43]

It's an astounding image to consider, rooted in New Testament thought: for here, at long last, is the Son of Adam and Eve who is not bound, enslaved, or "mastered" by the "power of death" (Acts 2:24; Heb. 2:14), and he has journeyed to the very depths of death to set his parents free.

WHILE WE CANNOT BE CERTAIN OF ALL THAT TOOK PLACE on Silent Saturday (and we must hold our opinions lightly), I think we can be certain of the truth that while Jesus' friends and followers were resting, he was making all things new.

Even though they did not know it, could not feel it, and dared not believe it, the power of death was being undone. Think about it: in the hour of their deepest discouragement, when the horrific events of Cross Friday had left them in a puddle of tears on Silent Saturday, it was then, smack dab in the middle of their searing pain, that God was already at work.

"Where can I go from your spirit?" the psalmist asks. "Or where can I flee from your presence? If I ascend to heaven [i.e., paradise], you are there; if I make my bed in Sheol [i.e., Hades], you are there . . ."

> If I say, "Surely the darkness shall cover me,
>   and the light around me become night,"
> even the darkness is not dark to you;
>   the night is as bright as the day,
>   for darkness is as light to you.
> —PSALM 139:7–12

You see, that's the thing about Jesus: whether it's paradise, prison, Hades, or hell, there's just nowhere, above or below, that he won't go to bring his lost brothers and sisters home.[44]

And more than anything else, that's what Silent Saturday is all about.

Ponder. What do you think was taking place on Silent Saturday?

Pray. Ask for the stubborn, stick-to-it, persevering faith to believe, to trust, to hold on during your day of deepest sorrow, smack dab in the middle of your most searing pain.

Practice. Consider rewriting Psalm 139:1–12 in your own words, making it as personal as possible—to guide, to comfort, to help you pray when all hope seems lost.

CHAPTER THIRTY-FOUR

"GOOD MORNING!"

*When the Sabbath was over, Mary Magdalene, Mary
the mother of James, and Salome bought spices so that they
could come and anoint Jesus. Then, very early on the first
day of the week, they came to the tomb, just at sunrise.
They were saying to one another, "There's that stone at the
door of the tomb—who's going to roll it away for us?"*

*Then, when they looked up, they saw that it had been
rolled away...*

—MARK 16:1–4

Mark is the shortest of the gospel accounts and has a brisk pace. It
includes lots of words and phrases like "straightaway," "that very
moment," "at once"—and those three examples are all in the first
chapter!

As a result, when it comes to the heart-skipping, history-altering
event of Sunday morning, Mark's record has the feel of a sudden shift
in the wind. It leaves you teetering on the edge of the unknown, still
trying to catch your breath, standing there with these three women,
in Mark's words, "totally astonished" (16:5).

Because an empty tomb wasn't at all what Jesus' friends and followers
were expecting.

I imagine that those brokenhearted and brave women who set out
early Sunday morning to embalm Jesus' dead body had practical matters

on their minds. I very much doubt that Mary, Mary, and Salome were thinking about Jesus' being like a grain of wheat that "falls into the earth and dies" before it produces "lots of fruit" (John 12:24).

No, it's much more likely these three women were thinking about the fact that Simon Peter and the other men were too afraid to come with them, and they had no idea how they would roll away the tomb's door. ("It was extremely large," Mark 16:4 tells us.)

"Then, when they looked up, they saw that it had been rolled away . . ."

Piecing together the various gospel accounts, it's difficult to follow the order of events as they unfold (an important and fascinating point that we'll explore in the next chapter), but without question the high point of this historic Sunday morning is when Jesus himself, in the flesh, encounters the women and says to them, apparently without a lot of fanfare, "Greetings!" (Matt. 28:9).

Or, even better, as Eugene Peterson translates it in *The Message*, "Good morning!"

IF JESUS REALLY DID DEFEAT DEATH, THEN JESUS REALLY IS King. More than anything, that is what Jesus' resurrection meant for his earliest friends and followers.

Because when Jesus was crucified, regardless of what he had explained to his disciples in advance, it meant only one thing to them: failure.

Another failed Messiah.

Another failed revolution.

Another failed attempt to change the world.

But when Jesus was raised from the dead—appearing first to the women, then to Simon Peter and the others, and in time to many more people—his resurrection meant:

Jesus is Messiah after all.

Which means the revolution is underway.

Which means the whole world is about to change.

Taking all of that into account, and keeping in mind that the women who first encountered the resurrected Jesus would become his first messengers, his first ambassadors, the very first good-news bringers of his death-defeating reign, you would think that King Jesus would greet them with something more than "Good morning!"

I mean, seriously, wouldn't it somehow be more appropriate or more regal to say something grand and elevated like, "Behold, I am the King!" Or maybe even just a straightforward, "Look, I'm alive!" But, no, Jesus says:

"Good morning!"

"Greetings!"

"Hi!"[45]

As if all of this makes perfect sense, as if all of this is somehow part of the plan.

Picture it: the King of all kings, having just defeated death and bearing the scars to prove it, looks into the eyes of these brave, terrified, trembling women and greets them in the most down-to-earth way possible, as if to say, "What, were you expecting someone else?"

After Jesus addresses them in this most wonderfully understated of ways, the gospel of Matthew goes on to explain that the women rushed to him, they fell to their knees, and they clung to him:

"Jesus said, 'You're holding on to me for dear life! Don't be frightened like that. Go tell my brothers that they are to go to Galilee, and that I'll meet them there'" (Matt. 28:10 *The Message*).

HAVING KNOWN THE STORY OF JESUS' RESURRECTION AS long as I can remember, it is hard for me to appreciate the delight his closest friends felt when they saw him alive—for them to look into his eyes and to feel the warmth of his skin, to hear the tone of Jesus' voice again.

This is where my precious kids have taught me so much.

When Bronwyn and I told our two oldest children, Miréa and Blaze, the story of how Jesus died, Miréa, with tears streaming, asked us the most important question of all: "Will God help Jesus? Will God give him his life back?"

It tore our hearts in two to let the question linger without resolution in our children's imagination for the night, but I'm so glad we did. Because the next morning, when we woke Miréa and Blaze with a surprise breakfast of pancakes and waffles and told them the incredible story of how those brave women went to take care of Jesus' dead body, but—to their great surprise!—they discovered that Jesus was alive and well, breathing and heart-beating, talking and smiling, it was as if hope itself walked into our home.

Miréa's sky-blue eyes went wide with wonder, and Blaze, my dear son, jumped up from his chair and started to run. (He couldn't help himself. The boy had to celebrate.) Miréa was after him in a flash, and they hugged and jumped, laughed and yelled loud enough for the whole of East Boston to hear, "He's alive! He's alive! He's alive!"

And for a brief and magical moment, seeing my children celebrate the resurrection with such abandon, I think I caught a glimpse of at least some of the delight, a little of the joy, the awe, the wonder that filled Jesus' earliest friends and followers when they saw him alive again for the first time.

The women went to take care of his dead body: to wash away the blood and grime, to weep over his death-wounds, to at least give his bruised and battered frame some semblance of dignity. To their astonishment, Jesus showed up to take care of *them* instead: to wipe away their tears, to undo their deepest sorrows, to let them know that the greatest enemy of all, death, had finally been defeated—and the very first thing the resurrected King Jesus said was, "Good morning!"

And it was.

Ponder. If Jesus really did defeat death, then what that means first and foremost is this: Jesus really is King.

Pray. Ask for the wild wonder of Jesus' resurrection to invade your heart and mind.

Practice. The next time you say, "Good morning," remember King Jesus on Easter day.

CHAPTER THIRTY-FIVE

SUNDAY RISING

*They went back, away from the tomb, and told all this to
the eleven and all the others. It was Mary Magdalene,
Joanna, and Mary the mother of James, and the others
with them. They said this to the apostles; and this message
seemed to them just stupid, useless talk, and they didn't
believe them.*

*Peter, though, got up and ran to the tomb. He stooped
down and saw only the grave-clothes. He went back home,
perplexed at what had happened.*

—LUKE 24:9–12

Everything turns on the resurrection of Jesus. Everything. If it didn't
actually happen, explains the apostle Paul, and we're just caught up in a
great, big myth (or, even worse, an outright lie), then "we are the most
pitiable members of the human race" (1 Cor. 15:19).

I think my son, Blaze, in his childlike way, understood the implications of Paul's statement when he asked me one day, "But *how* did God
give Jesus his life back, Dad? *How* did God raise him from the dead?"

(Good question, kid. You always make your dad go deeper.)

As far as I understand it, there are three (actually, four) essential
parts or aspects to the *how* of my son's question:

1. There's the historical *how*: Why should we believe God raised Jesus from the dead when we know that dead people stay dead?
2. There's the biological *how*: If God really did raise Jesus from the dead, what was and is the new biological body of Jesus like?
3. There's the theological *how*: On what theological terms did God raise Jesus from the dead, and why does it matter?
4. And finally, there's the why-does-all-of-this-make-a-difference-in-my-life *how*: How on earth (literally) do we put this into practice?

Please know that I didn't unpack all of this for my young son when he asked me his question. (Actually, I'm pretty sure I simply responded, "Good question, I'm not sure. Let's go ask your mom.")

But I am convinced that as we wrestle with these questions, our experience of being human can be transformed in the most powerful of ways.

And that's what these next few chapters are all about.

IF IT'S EVER BEEN CHALLENGING FOR YOU TO BELIEVE IN the resurrection of Jesus, don't worry, you're in good company. As it turns out, not one of Jesus' eleven disciples believed the initial report that he was alive, because it "seemed to them just stupid, useless talk" (Luke 24:11).

There are two good places to start when thinking about the historical nature of Jesus' resurrection: (1) the primary role of women in the accounts, and (2) the various and differing perspectives of the accounts.

First, one of the practical reasons the disciples did not trust the women's story is because they did not trust the *women*. In the ancient world, the testimony of a woman was not accepted in a court of law. First-century historian Josephus infamously said it like this: "From women let no evidence be accepted, because of the levity and flippancy of their gender."

Regardless of how much we may disagree with this shameful assessment of women, the important point is this: If a group of men in the first century wanted to make up a believable story about someone rising from the dead, they would not have chosen women as primary witnesses. But in every gospel account of the resurrection (all of those accounts written by first-century men), women are the first and cornerstone witnesses of the event.

That's a remarkable historical fact, plain and simple.

A second notable historical fact is that the various accounts of Jesus' resurrection do not necessarily agree on certain details. For example, was Mary Magdalene alone at the tomb, or was she with other women? Was there one angel, or were there two angels? When exactly did Simon Peter and his friend who "ran faster" than him go to the tomb (John 20:4)?

From a strictly historical angle, these minor differences in details make the central claim of the resurrection accounts more convincing, not less.[46]

Let me explain what I mean, using the criterion of dissimilarity.

About twenty-five years ago, my brother, Tré, and I, along with his best friend, Lance, broke a valuable porcelain figurine that belonged to a friend named Pam. There is no question as to whether the figurine was shattered. Everyone agrees on that point. But there are four slightly different versions about how it happened.

This is how it all took place: The porcelain figurine was perched on a table. The table was sitting behind a couch. Tré, Lance, and I were racing to that couch—and this is where things get a little fuzzy, because, to this day, Tré, Lance, and I all remember differently who landed on the couch first. But the main issue, as Pam made sure we understood, is that regardless of who hit the couch first, the couch then hit the table, which knocked the porcelain figurine from its perch, which resulted in its shattering into a thousand little pieces on the hard, wooden floor.[47]

The four of us each have our own perspective as to how that porcelain figurine was broken, not because it didn't happen but because it *did* happen—and the startling stories of the empty tomb and the resurrection of Jesus, each slightly different in certain, minor details, are a bit like that.

These first-century records don't read like historical conspiracy, as if a group of guys got together and said, "Let's come up with a really tight, well-crafted story about Jesus rising from the dead." No, these first-century documents read like they were written by people who experienced something real, something truly overwhelming, something that actually happened.

FOR THESE REASONS AND MANY MORE, ONE OF THE LEADING scholars of this period of ancient history, Géza Vermes of Oxford University, said it like this:

> When every argument has been considered and weighed, the only conclusion acceptable to the historian must be . . . interpretations of this one disconcerting fact: namely that the women who set out to pay their last respects to Jesus found to their consternation, not a body, but an empty tomb.[48]

The question of history, which is ultimately a question of faith, is this: Why was Jesus' tomb empty?

Maybe his friends stole the body. (But how would they make it past the Roman guards?) Maybe the guards stole the body. (But what would their motive be?) Maybe his disciples, because of their deep devotion, made up the whole story after he died. (But why didn't they make up stories that at least agreed on the basic things, like how many women were at the tomb, and, for that matter, why would these first-century men include women in the stories at all?)

For the disciples, what finally convinced them the women were telling the truth—that it wasn't "just stupid, useless talk"—was when they saw, touched, and talked with the resurrected Jesus themselves. (We will explore some of their incredible encounters with the risen King Jesus in the next few chapters.)

One final point, though, regarding the historical nature of the resurrection is the phenomenon that because Jesus was raised again on a Sunday, which in the ancient world was a working day, Sunday has been commemorated ever since by his followers as a day that is holy, a day to acknowledge and remember that death itself has been defeated, a day to celebrate his Sunday rising.[49]

Sunday wasn't simply the beginning of a new week for the earliest followers of Jesus. As we'll see in the next two chapters, it was the beginning of a whole new world.

Ponder. What do you think about the bodily resurrection of Jesus? Do you believe it happened? If so, why? If not, why not?

Pray. When it comes to your doubts about the historical reality of the resurrection, pray like the man in Mark 9:24, who cried, "I believe! Help me in my unbelief!"

Practice. Remember the resurrection of Jesus this Sunday and, if you believe, then celebrate his Sunday rising well.

CHAPTER THIRTY-SIX

BIOLOGY 2.0

As they were saying this, Jesus himself stood in the midst of them, and said "Peace be with you." They were terrified and alarmed, and thought they were seeing a ghost.
"Why are you so disturbed?" he said. "Why do these questionings come up in your hearts? Look at my hands and feet; it really is me, myself. Touch me and see! Ghosts don't have flesh and bones like you can see I have."
—LUKE 24:36–39

Like us, the ancients had a heartfelt and tantalizing attachment to ghost stories. The most well known of these stories in Jewish history is the peculiar tale of King Saul consulting a medium to "bring up" the "spirit" of the dead prophet Samuel (1 Sam. 28:8).

With that kind of thing in mind, it makes sense that when the disciples encounter the resurrected Jesus, they assume he is an apparition, maybe a phantom or wraith—you know, the Ghost of Jesus Past come to visit them from the grave.

Jesus, realizing what his disciples are thinking, quickly provides them with a lesson in human biology. "Look at my hands and feet; it really is me, myself. Touch me and see!" he says. "Ghosts don't have flesh and bones like you can see I have."

No, this wasn't a phantom or a ghost, a mirage, a specter, a spirit, an apparition, a vision, or a collective experience of spiritual hysteria induced by a severely traumatic event or postmortem grief. According to numerous eyewitness accounts, this was Jesus—in the flesh—and you could touch him.

As you might imagine, the overwhelmed disciples are "still in disbelief and amazement," so Jesus does the most disarming and down-to-earth thing he could possibly do. He asks for some food:

"'Have you got something here to eat?' They gave him a piece of baked fish, which he took and ate in front of them" (Luke 24:41–43).

Think about it: Jesus has just defeated death, proving he really is the Messiah, and he's now about to launch a global movement to transform the entire planet, but first, just to show that he really is human, he asks his bewildered disciples for a quick bite to eat to demonstrate that he can chew, swallow, and digest food just like the rest of us. (How can you not love this man?)

EACH OF THE GOSPEL ACCOUNTS REFERS TO VARIOUS aspects of Jesus' resurrected body, but the gospel of Luke and the gospel of John provide some interesting details about the perplexing biology of it all:

- *One of the most peculiar aspects of Jesus' resurrected body is that sometimes he is immediately recognized, but other times he is not.* Even more peculiar, perhaps, is that the risen Jesus seems to enjoy using this phenomenon to his advantage. For example, the gospel of Luke tells a story of the resurrected Jesus walking and talking with two disciples whose eyes "were prevented from recognizing him." Jesus, it says, gives them "the impression that he was going further" (he's acting!) so that they will invite him to stay for a meal. Then, as Jesus is breaking bread for dinner, powerfully reminiscent of the Last Supper, their eyes "were opened" to him (24:13–32).
- *Jesus' resurrected body is not bound by place and space.* According

to the gospel of Luke, immediately after Jesus breaks bread with the two disciples, "he vanished from their sight" (24:31). The two disciples race to find the rest of the disciples to tell them all about it, and, suddenly, Jesus is there "in the midst of them" (24:36). When the gospel of John recounts this story in a different way, we are told that "the doors were shut" when "Jesus came and stood in the middle of them" (20:19). Jesus somehow passed through the doors.

- *The resurrected body of Jesus, while not bound by place and space, is still solid.* Remember, Jesus' resurrected body can be touched, and the risen Jesus breaks bread and eats fish. At the same time, though, Jesus passes through locked doors "like you and I walk through the morning mist."[50] In that sense, the risen and transformed body of Jesus seems to be even more solid than the door—the door was like vapor to him. (C. S. Lewis's enjoyable and insightful book *The Great Divorce* has influenced me more than any other work when it comes to imagining just how incredibly solid the resurrected body of Jesus is.)

- *Finally, and maybe most surprising of all, the resurrected body of Jesus still carries its death scars.* While Jesus' body has been transformed in the most amazing and marvelous of ways, the gospel of Luke and the gospel of John make it plain that the scars from his crucifixion remain. "Bring your finger here," Jesus tells his friend and disciple Thomas, who is struggling to believe that Jesus truly has been raised from the dead, "and inspect my hands. Bring your hand here and put it into my side" (John 20:27). The nail marks in Jesus' hands and feet, the place where the spear was plunged into his side, these scars, like some sort of sacred and eternal sign of his battle against and victory over sin and death, are still there.

So even as Jesus provides his disciples with a basic lesson in Biology 1.0 by showing that he can do physical things like break bread and eat fish, at the same time he's giving them an advanced course in Biology 2.0. Because the resurrected Jesus is also doing things that are well outside our understanding of what a physical body should be able to do, like vanishing from one place and appearing in another, and passing right through solid doors.

THE RESURRECTION OF THE BODY WAS A DEFINING BELIEF for the first followers of Jesus. So much so that the early Christian practice of baptism (being "buried" under the water, and then "raised up" from that water) was meant to identify the convert with Jesus' death and resurrection (Rom. 6:3–5).

The apostle Paul, though, takes this resurrection conviction much farther than symbolism or even sacrament when he explains that what happened to Jesus' body will, in time, take place with our bodies too. "Our present body is a shabby old thing," the apostle writes in Philippians 3:21, "but he's going to transform it so that it's just like his glorious body."

Let those words get into you: just like his glorious body.

It's a stunning, awe-inspiring idea—that one day, in the same way Jesus' broken body was made new, our bodies will be transformed too.

Does that mean, for example, new spinal cords for those suffering from paraplegia? Yes, it does. Does that mean new limbs for those born without arms? Yes, that's exactly what it means. Does that mean our bodies will not necessarily be bound by the limitations we now know? Yes, yes, yes, I certainly hope that's what it means!

"For God is not simply mending," explains C. S. Lewis in *Miracles*, "not simply restoring a status quo. Redeemed humanity is to be something [even] more glorious than unfallen humanity . . ."[51]

But this is not just a wildly inspiring hope for us and for our bodies. It is also a wildly inspiring hope for those who have died before us.

The resurrection of our bodies means that my wife, Bronwyn, who lost her father to cancer when she was fifteen years old, will get to see her dad again. Not just a ghostly apparition or the soul of her father, mind you. Bronwyn will get to *hug* her father again. She will be able to hold his hand, touch his face, and maybe even introduce him to his grandkids (and his son-in-law) for the very first time.

Resurrection means that in Jesus there is hope for those who have lost friends and even children to tragic events, whether to a shooting in urban America or a bombing in war-torn Syria. Because in Jesus there is hope that the suffering of such heartbreaking, life-altering tragedies can be transformed by new, resurrection life.

While the scriptures are not clear as to how such miraculous things will take place (yet another deep and bewildering mystery of Biology 2.0), they are abundantly clear that such amazing things *will* take place, all because of the bodily resurrection of Jesus—and, wow, I can hardly wait.

Ponder. "We've been given a glimpse of the real thing . . . our resurrection bodies! The Spirit of God whets our appetite by giving us a taste of what's ahead. He puts a little of heaven in our hearts so that we'll never settle for less" (2 Cor. 5:4–5 *The Message*).

Pray. Ask that the hope of resurrection in Jesus will inform and transform your view of death, that it will comfort you in great loss and enable you to live without fear.

Practice. Stop stressing so much about the physical things you don't like about yourself, trusting that all will be transformed in time. "Instead," in the words of Jesus, "make your top priority God's kingdom and his way of life . . ." (Matt. 6:33).

CHAPTER THIRTY-SEVEN

THE GARDENER

"Woman," Jesus said to her, "why are you crying? Who are
you looking for?"
   She guessed he must be the gardener.
   "Sir," she said, "if you've carried him off somewhere,
tell me where you've put him, and I will take him away."
   "Mary!" said Jesus.
   She turned and spoke in Aramaic.
   "Rabbouni!" she said (which means "Teacher").
                                         —JOHN 20:15–16

Of all the resurrection accounts in the gospel narratives, it is the tender way Jesus and Mary Magdalene interact in this scene that impacts me the most.

First, there is Mary, so devoted to Jesus and so devastated by his death that she must at least be near his dead body. She must at least care for her friend and teacher in his death in a way she was unable to in the final moments of his life. But when Mary arrives at the garden tomb, she discovers the doorway wide open and Jesus' body no longer there. Not knowing what else to do, "Mary stood outside the tomb, crying . . ." (John 20:11).

Then, there is King Jesus, standing beside her, even before Mary realizes someone is there. "Why are you crying?" he asks her. "Who are you looking for?" Has there ever been a more sensitive and searching question?

Mary assumes this stranger (apparently the gardener) must know something about Jesus, must have seen something, must be able to tell her where she can find his body, so she pleads with him. "Sir," she says, "if you've carried him off somewhere, tell me where you've put him, and I will take him away."

"Mary," the gardener speaks.

And the whole earth becomes quiet, completely still, because Mary recognizes that voice. She recognizes the way Jesus says her name.

"Rabbouni!" she cries in response.

AFTER EDEN AND AFTER GETHSEMANE COMES A THIRD garden in the story of God. The gospel of John emphasizes that the resurrection took place in a garden because John, more than any other gospel account, wants you to understand the cosmic theological significance of the resurrection of Jesus.

According to John, in the same way that Adam and Eve were given charge of the old creation in the garden of Eden, the resurrected King Jesus (i.e., the Gardener) has now been given charge of the new creation in a new garden.*

The theological terms of this vital exchange, according to the apostle Paul, are fairly straightforward: "All die in Adam, you see, and all will be made alive in the Messiah" (1 Cor. 15:22). Using similar imagery, but unpacking the concept even further, Paul says it like this in his letter to the Romans:

> If one man's sin put crowds of people at the dead-end abyss of separation from God, just think what God's gift poured through one man, Jesus Christ, will do! There's no comparison between that death-dealing sin and this generous, life-giving gift. The verdict on

---

* John sets this amazing Genesis-to-Jesus parallel in place when he begins his gospel account by quoting the opening words of the book of Genesis, "In the beginning . . ." (John 1:1).

that one sin was the death sentence; the verdict on the many sins that followed was this wonderful life sentence. If death got the upper hand through one man's wrongdoing, can you imagine the breathtaking recovery life makes, sovereign life, in those who grasp with both hands this wildly extravagant life-gift, this grand setting-everything-right, that the one man Jesus Christ provides? (Rom. 5:15–17 *The Message*)

According to Paul, the theological terms on which God raised Jesus from the dead are rooted in the rich soil of the garden of Eden, where Adam and Eve, the prototype of every son and every daughter of the earth, were given a clear command and an accompanying consequence. "You may freely eat of every tree of the garden," God told them, "but of the tree of the knowledge of good and evil you shall not eat, for in the day that you eat of it you shall die" (Gen. 2:16–17).

And die they did, just as humans have died ever since—including Jesus.

Because the fruit of that tree was infected with sin, shiny on the outside but crawling with worms all the way to the core. When Adam and Eve devoured that fruit, it produced death in humankind, and that sin-diseased, death-producing way of being human ruled the earth until Jesus.

But Jesus—whom the apostle Paul calls the "Last Adam" (1 Cor. 15:45)—did not touch, taste, or eat the fruit of sin, ever.

So even though he lived in the dire sin-diseased brokenness of our humanity and suffered its cruelest and most inhumane consequences in his crucifixion, King Jesus was not bound by its death-effecting power.

The power of death could not contain, control, or master King Jesus because the sovereignty of sin had no claim over his life. Sin and death did not rule him. The book of Hebrews says it like this:

Since the children [that's us!] share in blood and flesh, he too shared in them, in just the same way, so that through death he might destroy the one who has the power of death—that is, the devil—and set free the people who all their lives long were under the power of slavery because of the fear of death. (Heb. 2:14–15)

Because of the resurrection of Jesus—and the sure and solid hope of our own—death has now been defeated, dismantled, exhausted, which means we have nothing to fear! Or as the apostle Paul puts it:

> Death swallowed by triumphant Life!
> Who got the last word, oh, Death?
> Oh, Death, who's afraid of you now?
> —1 CORINTHIANS 15:54–55 *THE MESSAGE*

THE GOSPEL OF JOHN AND ITS GENESIS-JESUS MESSAGE IS not yet done. Because soon after Jesus encounters Mary in the garden, he does something significant and profoundly symbolic to his disciples, something that any attentive reader of the book of Genesis would immediately recognize:

> "Peace be with you," Jesus said to them again. "As the father has sent me, so I'm sending you."
> With that, he *breathed* on them.
> "Receive the holy spirit," he said. (John 20:21–22, italics added)

This is a breathtaking moment (pun most definitely intended), and its message could not be any clearer:

In the same way that God breathed life into humanity in the old creation, Jesus is now breathing the life of Holy Spirit into the humanity of this new creation.

"From this moment on, therefore" the apostle Paul says in 2 Corinthians 5:16–17, "we don't regard anybody from a merely human point of view. Even if we once regarded the Messiah that way, we don't do so any longer. Thus, if anyone is in the Messiah, there is a new creation! Old things have gone, and look—everything has become new!"

When it comes to the world-changing theology of the resurrection of Jesus, we're not just talking about a new religion, a new philosophy, or a three-step plan to make sure you get into heaven after you die. We are talking about a new way to be human, a way that lives and breathes like King Jesus.*

Ponder. The power of death could not contain, control, or master King Jesus because the sovereignty of sin had no claim over his life.

Pray. Ask that you will be able to say, like King Jesus did, that the devil "has nothing on me, no claim on me" (John 14:30 *The Message*).

Practice. Examine your life, especially your relationships and routines, and ask the Holy Spirit to show you any area in which the sovereignty of sin is ruling over you.

---

* If you're going to read only one book (other than the gospel accounts) about the resurrection of Jesus and what it means for humans, for the planet, and for the future, then make it N. T. Wright's *Surprised by Hope: Rethinking Heaven, the Resurrection and the Mission of the Church* (New York: HarperOne, 2008).

CHAPTER THIRTY-EIGHT

NEW RULES FOR
A NEW WORLD

*After this, Jesus showed himself again to the disciples by the
sea of Tiberias. This was how he showed himself.*

*Simon Peter, Thomas (known as Didymus), Nathanael
from Cana in Galilee, the sons of Zebedee, and two other
disciples were all together.*

Simon Peter spoke up.

"I'm going fishing," he said.

"We'll go with you," they replied.

*So they went off and got into the boat; but that night
they caught nothing.*

As dawn was breaking, Jesus stood beside the seashore . . .

—JOHN 21:1–4

"If you don't play by the world's rules," a wise friend once told me,
"then you don't have to play by the world's rules." If you don't bow to
the world's system (the world's way of doing things), then you are not
bound to the world's system (the world's way of getting things).

Remember, even though the rule of sin and death led to Jesus'
crucifixion, King Jesus was not bound by that power because he never
played by its rules.

So the pressing question is this: How do we live like that in the here and now, while we wait for and anticipate our own resurrection, for the "redemption of our body" as it's described in Romans 8:23?

How on earth (again, literally) do we put the kingdom into practice here? What does this resurrected-King-Jesus way of living and being look like in the nitty-gritty of our nine-to-five lives, in the real-world realities of interacting with our neighbors next door, and in the day-to-day concerns of caring for our family and friends?

Thankfully, the final resurrection appearance in the gospel of John shows us exactly how, and to that extraordinarily ordinary moment we now turn.

MOST SURPRISING ABOUT THIS FINAL RESURRECTION appearance in John is its context. It's not like when Mary Magdalene was weeping outside the garden tomb or like when the disciples were hiding behind locked doors. No, this resurrection appearance takes place when seven of the boys are just out doing what they know how to do (and what they probably love to do): fishing.

Various Bible commentators suggest the reason the disciples decide to go fishing in this story is because they desired to return to their old way of living, their pre-Jesus way of being, before he called them to start "fishing for people" (Mark 1:17). But I don't think that's the case. I think Peter and his pals go fishing in this story because they are fishermen, because that's what they do and that's how they eat. Fishing was simply how they provided for themselves and for their families.

And then—*bam!*—the resurrected King Jesus shows up unexpectedly, right in the middle of a normal work day, and suggests they try fishing his way:

"Children," said Jesus to them, "have you got anything to eat?"

"No!" they replied.

"Cast the net on the right side of the boat," he said, "and you'll find something."

So they cast the net; and now they couldn't draw it in because of the weight of the fish. (John 21:5–6)

We'll come back to this point, but for now, remember this: in this story King Jesus doesn't ask the disciples to stop being fishermen—he just transforms the way they fish.

THE GOSPEL OF JOHN RECORDS THAT WHEN SIMON PETER realizes it's Jesus on the seashore, he "threw himself into the sea" (21:7). Bold, brave, audacious Peter simply cannot wait for the boat to get to Jesus, so he sets out swimming instead.

When everyone else finally arrives, they discover that King Jesus has breakfast on the beach ready and waiting for them. Everything is prepared.

Apparently, Jesus has already caught a few fish himself this morning (just think about that: the resurrected King Jesus went fishing!) and those fish, as well as some bread, are cooking on the charcoal fire when the disciples show up. Jesus adds a few of the disciples' fresh catch to the fire and then says to the boys, "Come and have breakfast" (John 21:9–12).

Wow, breakfast on the beach with the resurrected King Jesus: if ever there was a glimpse of what the down-to-earth "new heaven and new earth" of Revelation 21 might be like, surely this is it.

After Jesus and the boys have had their fill of breakfast, Jesus turns his attention to Simon Peter. While there is so much that could be said about the depth of the conversation Jesus and Peter share in this honest and vulnerable moment, the most important thing to know is that Jesus provides Simon Peter with the opportunity to reaffirm his commitment to him three times, the same number of times that Peter had earlier denied him (John 21:15–19).

Jesus refuses to allow Peter's mistakes—as painful and as shameful as they are—to determine his dear friend's destiny and calling. Again, we'll come back to this important point, but for now, remember this: King Jesus exposes the deepest sin and sorrow of Peter's heart, and then sets him free from its condemnation.

FINALLY, ONCE PETER IS FREE, REINSTATED, AND PRO-foundly aware of his calling, Jesus lets Peter know that he, like his king, will die for the cause of the kingdom (John 21:18–19).* Peter was never afraid to ask questions (such an admirable trait), so when Jesus tells him the manner in which he will die, Peter asks about another disciple:

> "Master," said Peter to Jesus . . . "what about him?"
>
> "If it's my intention," replied Jesus, "that he should remain here until I come, what's that got to do with you? You must follow me!" (21:21–22)

It is here that Jesus helps Simon Peter (and the rest of us too) understand one of the most important principles or rules of this new world, this new creation that had its start in the resurrection of Jesus: judgment belongs to King Jesus alone, and we must never compare ourselves or our calling with others.

SO THEN HOW DOES ALL OF THIS WORK IN THE HERE AND now? How do we put the resurrection of Jesus into practice while we wait for our own?

1. *Expect the presence of Jesus in your day-to-day activities and be prepared to change how you do things when he shows up.*

---

* When the gospel of John was written, the apostle Peter was already dead, providing a real sense of poignancy to the author's memory of Peter in this moment. According to tradition, Simon Peter was crucified like Jesus, but when the executioners came for him, he requested to be crucified upside-down because he felt unworthy to die in the same manner as his king.

We cannot script what King Jesus will ask of us, but, for instance, in business it means that your "bottom line" most likely will become something more than just profit.

2. *Expect King Jesus to reveal, forgive, and heal your deepest sin and sorrow.* This process could be painful, like a surgeon taking a scalpel to your body before anesthesia has taken effect. But know this: if sin's cancer is not removed from you, it will not relent until it destroys you.

3. *Stop judging and comparing yourself with others.* This is one of the most entrenched evils of the human condition, how we gauge our worthiness or unworthiness by our skewed view of others. You have one responsibility today: to follow Jesus, as best you know how, in what is set before you.

Whenever we live by these new rules (in our family life, in our careers, in our neighborhoods), we can anticipate this new-world resurrection power of King Jesus to be present in our activities, knowing that nothing—*nothing!*—that we do in Jesus will be in vain (1 Cor. 15:58).

Ponder. What area of your life (job, school, family, etc.) is most in need of the presence and power of Jesus?

Pray. Ask for the eyes of your heart, your mind, and your will to be open and attentive to the unexpected presence of King Jesus in your day-to-day activities and responsibilities.

Practice. Consider writing these words down and putting them somewhere prominent as a daily reminder: "I have one responsibility today—to follow Jesus, as best I know how, in what God has set before me."

CHAPTER THIRTY-NINE

ASCENSION

*He took them out as far as Bethany, and lifted up his
hands and blessed them. As he was blessing them, he was
separated from them and carried into heaven.*
—LUKE 24:50–51

*Then, lo and behold, two men appeared, dressed in white,
standing beside them.*
*"Galileans," they said, "why are you standing here
staring into heaven? This Jesus, who has been taken from
you into heaven, will come back in the same way you saw
him go into heaven."*
—ACTS 1:10–11

The bodily ascension of the resurrected Jesus and what it means for
you, for me, and for the whole of humanity is one of the most underappreciated and least understood truths of the gospel.

It's a peculiar, unprecedented scene to be sure, seemingly almost
too strange to be true. But there it is, like a first-century take on a
twenty-first-century science-fiction film, the resurrected Jesus being
transported into another realm, "lifted up" into another dimension,
"carried into heaven" (Acts 1:9; Luke 24:51).

Particularly interesting to me is that right alongside the strangeness
of it all is the rawness of it, because it's certainly not as if the earliest

believers have all of their Jesus-and-God theology sorted out by now. They are still very much trying to understand what all of this means.

For example, in the gospel of Matthew, just moments before the resurrected Jesus charges his closest disciples with the Great Commission, the narrative says that they "worshipped him, though some *hesitated*" (28:17, italics added).

Yes, you read that right: the disciples, a full forty days after Jesus' resurrection and just before his bodily ascension into heaven, still hesitated in their worship of Jesus. (And, just so it's clear, most of us would have hesitated too!) It's not as if there was a Jesus-Is-God Roadmap for the disciples to follow.

This was uncharted territory.

THE GOSPEL OF LUKE AND THE BOOK OF ACTS ARE A TWO-volume work, written by the same ancient author and intended as one narrative, and it is in reading these works together that we see how the earliest friends and followers of Jesus begin to understand his identity in a whole new way.

Just before Jesus ascends, he commissions his disciples in two ways: (1) he tells them about the work of resurrection witnessing that is now set before them, and (2) he instructs them to wait in Jerusalem until they are equipped with Holy Spirit power for this worldwide mission (Luke 24:45–49; Acts 1:3–8).

(I should mention here that Acts 1:4 makes it wonderfully clear that all of this instruction takes place "as they were having a meal together"—oh yes, how the resurrected Jesus continues to enjoy dining with his closest friends!)

While the gospel of Luke (in what the author describes as his "previous book" in Acts 1:1) recounts what "Jesus *began* to do and teach," it is understood that the book of Acts is now recounting what Jesus *continues* to do and teach through his "chosen apostles" (Acts 1:1–2, italics added).

After an explosive introduction in the second chapter of Acts, including the windlike filling of the Holy Spirit, resulting in "tongues, seemingly made of fire" resting on "each one of them," Luke explains that "they were all filled with the holy spirit and began to speak in other languages . . ." (Acts 2:1–4).

The historic result of this dynamic infilling of the Holy Spirit is that Simon Peter boldly embraces his calling and announces the message of King Jesus' life, death, and resurrection to all who are gathered in Jerusalem. "About three thousand people were added to the community that day," the story continues. "They all gave their full attention to the teaching of the apostles and to the common life, to the breaking of bread and the prayers" (Acts 2:41–42).

Through various ups and downs, recounted in numerous amazing stories as well as in some challenging circumstances, the book of Acts continues in this way until a turning point takes place in chapter seven. While the details are far too many to recount here, the decisive shift centers on a follower of Jesus named Stephen, a man "filled with grace and power" (Acts 6:8).

According to the narrative, Stephen—like Jesus, mind you—begins saying some controversial things about the Temple, things that in time land Stephen in the same hot seat as Jesus, on trial before the Temple authorities. "What do you have to say for yourself?" he is asked by the high priest (Acts 7:1 *The Message*).

Apparently, that was just the question Stephen was hoping to be asked, because once he starts responding, Stephen does not stop speaking for fifty-five verses, and the only reason he stops then is because the Temple authorities have him killed (Acts 7:57–60).

The primary reason that Stephen is killed is because at the high point of his message he has a vision and cries, "I can see heaven opened, and the son of man standing at God's right hand" (Acts 7:56).

Does that language, that message, that title—Son of Man—sound familiar at all?

It should, because it's the same language and same title that leads to the charge of blasphemy in Jesus' trial, and it's through Jesus' bodily ascension that his role as the Son of Man is at last understood.

STEPHEN DOESN'T SEE A SPIRIT OR AN ANGEL AT THE RIGHT hand of God, he sees a human, and that human, the risen King Jesus, is ruling alongside the "Ancient One," in the words of the prophet Daniel:

> I saw one like a human being [again, the literal translation is
> "son of man"] coming with the clouds of heaven.
> And he came to the Ancient One
> and was presented before him.
> To him was given dominion
> and glory and kingship,
> that all peoples, nations, and languages
> should serve him.
> His dominion is an everlasting dominion
> that shall not pass away,
> and his kingship is one
> that shall never be destroyed.
> —DANIEL 7:13–14

It is on this decidedly Jewish and radical theological foundation that the earliest apostles understand Jesus' identity in accordance with his own description of himself—as the Son of the Father.

In time, because of Jesus' words (which provide astounding new light to foundational, incarnational Jewish beliefs about Torah and Temple, among other things), and also because of an ever-deepening understanding in the Holy Spirit, the first apostles at long last see the very being of God through the relational lens of Father, Son, and Holy Spirit.*

---

* For example, the mysterious plurality of "Let *us* make humankind in *our* image" of Genesis 1:26 is now seen in brilliant, beautiful new light through the lens of Jesus' words in Matthew 28:19, "in the name of the *father*, and of the *son*, and of the *holy spirit*" (italics added).

I realize all of that is quite a mouthful, but, in my own estimation, it was in this way that the earliest friends and followers of Jesus ultimately arrived at the astonishing conviction that in seeing Jesus, we have seen the human face of God.

Now, lest we become overwhelmed by the sheer magnitude of it all, let me do my best to state as clearly as I can what the bodily ascension of the resurrected King Jesus means right now:

It means there is "one like a human being" ruling with God, right now.

It means that that one is made of flesh and blood and bones, right now.

It means that one day you will meet this God-human, King Jesus, in the flesh.

We will be able to see Jesus, touch Jesus, and—yes!—even enjoy food with Jesus.

And just in case you are wondering how we will know that it really, truly is him: Don't worry, you'll know it's him, because only King Jesus will still have scars.

Ponder. One day, you will meet Jesus in the flesh, heart-beating and breathing, walking and talking, ruling and reigning: King Jesus.

Pray. Ask that you will be ready for that day: "For we must all appear before the judgment seat of the Messiah, so that each may receive what has been done through the body, whether good or bad" (2 Cor. 5:10).

Practice. If you are fearful of that day for any reason, then put these words into practice right now: "If you profess with your mouth that Jesus is Lord, and believe in your heart that God raised him from the dead, you will be saved . . . The Bible says, you see, 'Everyone who believes in him will not be put to shame.'" (Rom. 10:9–11).

CHAPTER FORTY

IN THE BEGINNING

There are many other things which Jesus did.
If they were written down one by one, I don't think the
world itself would be able to contain the books that would
be written.

—JOHN 21:25

Matthew, Mark, Luke, and John begin their gospel accounts in different ways. The gospel of Matthew, for example, begins by tracing the genealogy of Jesus all the way back to Abraham and Sarah, the mother and father of the Jewish people (1:1). Matthew does this because he wants us to know that the story of Jesus he is telling is a distinctly Jewish story: it's the story of the King of the Jews.

The gospel of Luke, on the other hand, traces the genealogy of Jesus even farther back, all the way to Adam and Eve, the mother and father of humanity (3:23–38). What Luke is saying in this unique genealogy is this: The story of Jesus I am telling you is not just a Jewish story. This is a story for the whole of humankind.

But the gospel of John is different, decidedly so.

Because John, with echoes of the opening words of Genesis reverberating through his heart and mind, traces the genealogy of Jesus all the way back to "In the beginning . . ." (1:1). It's nearly impossible, two thousand years later in another culture, language, and setting, to even begin to grasp what John has just done.

What John is saying is this: The story of Jesus I am telling you is not just a Jewish story or a human story. The story of Jesus is the story of God.

There's an old Hebrew word—*chutzpah*—that best describes what is taking place when John begins his story about Jesus this way. *Chutzpah* is used to describe a type of thinking or behaviour that is brazen, outrageous, even dangerous, and I simply cannot tell you what sort of *chutzpah* John requires to begin his gospel account about Jesus in the same way as the book of Genesis.

But the gospel of John does not stop there. John goes on to say that this Jesus—the "Word" who was "In the beginning" and through whom "all things came into existence . . ."—this "Word became flesh and lived among us. We gazed upon his glory," John says, "glory like that of the father's only son . . ." (1:1–14).

Seriously, try your best to take a step back from two thousand years of Christian history, tradition, and culture and imagine what it was like for the earliest believers to begin saying that in seeing Jesus—their teacher, healer, friend, and king—they had seen the humanity of God.

Now, that's some serious *chutzpah*.

THERE ARE THREE GREAT TRUTHS ON WHICH JUST ABOUT everything else in Christianity rests: the Trinity, the incarnation, and the ascension. (And just so it's clear, the incarnation speaks not just of the Son becoming human at his birth but of the whole of his human life—his birth, life, death, resurrection, and beyond.)

While it would take another book (and then some) to explore these God realities as they unfold throughout the Bible, I'll do my best (with the help of a wise and down-to-earth theologian) to briefly articulate in a few paragraphs why these truths are so important:

- *The Trinity means that when we say God, we are saying Father, Son, and Holy Spirit.* "God is not some faceless, all-powerful abstraction," explains theologian Baxter Kruger in his wonderfully accessible book *The Great Dance*. "God is Father, Son and Spirit, existing in a passionate and joyous fellowship."[52]

The very being of God is relational: picture a vibrant, never-ending, life-giving dance shared by Father, Son, and the Holy Spirit. And the vital and glorious reason that you and I and the entire cosmos were created is so that we would enter that dance. Or, as Paul puts it, that we would be "adopted as sons and daughters" into God's family (Eph. 1:5).

• *The incarnation means that, in the Son, the life of the Triune God has become human.* How else would the life of God—this great and eternal dance of Father, Son, and Holy Spirit—reach humanity unless "at least one of the Trinity enters into our world and becomes what we are"?[53]

The Son's becoming one of us was not a divine afterthought or emergency plan B to deal with the consequences of sin. No, the Triune God "chose us in him before the world was made . . . that's what gave him delight," Paul explains in Ephesians. "His plan was to sum up the whole cosmos in the king—yes, everything in heaven and on earth, in him" (1:4–10).

• *The ascension means the Son is still human, right now.* The dance of God "is no longer just a divine dance. It is now and forever a divine-human dance," and it is through Jesus, the one who became and who will always be human, that we are now welcomed into that dance too.[54]

"Because of this," Paul says, "I am kneeling down before the father, the one who gives the name of 'family' to every family there is, in heaven and on earth. My prayer is this: that he will lay out all the riches of his glory to give you strength and power, through his spirit, in your inner being: that the king may make his home in your hearts . . ." (Eph. 3:14–17).

King Jesus, we must understand, did not temporarily become human just to fix the sin problem. No! The Son took on flesh and blood, now and forever, because it is God's eternal purpose for the sons and daughters of the earth—that's us!—to be welcomed in, to enter the dance, to be adopted into the family of God.

"It was not the Fall of Adam," explains Baxter Kruger, "that set God's agenda; it was the decision to share the great dance with us through Jesus." He continues:

> [Jesus] became human to accomplish the eternal purpose of our adoption, and in order to bring our adoption to pass, the Fall had to be called to a halt and undone. The catastrophe of Adam certainly made the road of incarnation, and thus of our adoption, one of pain and suffering and death, but it did not create its necessity. Jesus is not a footnote to Adam and his fall; the Fall, and indeed creation itself, is a footnote to the purpose of God in Jesus Christ.[55]

THE GOSPEL OF JOHN WAS THE LAST OF THE GOSPEL accounts to be written, and it wraps up in the most mysterious and hopeful of ways.

Just after the resurrected King Jesus shows up while the boys are fishing, after he prepares breakfast on the beach for them, after he makes sure that his dear friend and disciple Simon Peter knows that everything is forgiven, John completes the story of Jesus' life, death, and resurrection by writing:

> There are many other things which Jesus did. If they were written down one by one, I don't think the world itself would be able to contain the books that would be written. (John 21:25)

Personally, I don't think John is talking about a bunch of miracles that Jesus did during his hidden years or something conspiratorial like that, because, remember, John has the creation account of Genesis in mind all the way through his gospel.

In this peculiar, closing passage, I think John is giving us a glimpse into the mysterious purpose and meaning behind creation itself. I think he's tearing back the fabric of our fallen ways, the thick cloud of our sin-diseased humanity that is forever trying to eclipse the eternal purposes of God with the personal drama of our sin, and he's pointing us toward the reason that humans were made in the first place.

"The whole dance, or drama, or pattern of this three-Person life," C. S. Lewis says of the Father, Son, and Holy Spirit in *Mere Christianity*, "is to be played out in each one of us: or (putting it the other way around) each one of us has got to enter that pattern, take his place in that dance."[56]

Genesis tells us we were made in the image of God, and I believe what Lewis is suggesting here and what John is getting at in his surprising, mysterious, to-be-continued closing of "many other things which Jesus did" is that—in Jesus—there is far more to being human than we can possibly imagine.

Fishing and farming and football, painting a picture or planting a garden, parenting our children or writing a book, serving the "least of these" or suffering for our faith, fighting injustice or falling madly in love, chopping onions before dinner or having breakfast on the beach—because of the resurrected and ascended King Jesus, such things are even now reflecting the life, the creativity, the compassion, the joy of eternal relationship that is Father, Son, and Holy Spirit.

After all, humans are made in the image of God, aren't we?

So the next time you are out fishing, or whatever it is that fills your made-in-the-image-of-God-each-and-every-day human existence, be on the lookout for the risen King Jesus. Because, truly, he just might show up and transform your ordinary, average, run-of-the-mill day into yet another amazing part of the unfolding story of God, the "many other things which Jesus did."

Ponder. Because of Jesus, fishing and farming, cleaning and creating, parenting and working—the ordinary stuff of what it means to be human—these things will never ever be the same.

Pray. Take some time, right now if you can, to get down on your knees, to lift your hands high, or maybe even to dance and give thanks for the "wildly extravagant life-gift" of God in King Jesus (Rom. 5:17 *The Message*).

Practice. Today, live in the awe-inspiring awareness that God—the one whose face we have seen in Jesus—knows exactly what it means to be human.

EPILOGUE

"Just show us the Father, then, Master," said Philip to
Jesus, "and that'll be good enough for us!"
*   "Have I been with you for such a long time, Philip,"*
replied Jesus, "and still you don't know me? Anyone who
has seen me has seen the father!"
—JOHN 14:8–9

"I've said all this to you while I'm here with you. But the
helper, the holy spirit, the one the father will send in my
name, he will teach you everything. He will bring back to
your mind everything I've said to you."
—JOHN 14:25–26

A few weeks ago, as a number of our neighborhood friends and their children were piling into our East Boston home for house church, my son, Blaze, helped me realize something important about Jesus, the Father, and the Holy Spirit.

It happened when our dear friends Jenn and Davis Droll showed up, along with their precocious and curly-haired four-year-old son, Nathan. I was still in my study when they arrived, but I caught a glimpse of Nathan as he raced by the study's doorway to join his buddy Blaze in the living room.

When I saw young Nathan, I knew Davis and Jenn must be here as well, and I playfully called to Blaze, "Hey, who's here?"

It was my son's response that caught me off guard.

I'm so accustomed to interacting with the Droll family as one that I just assumed he would respond, "It's the Drolls!"

But Blaze, with every ounce of enthusiasm he had, cried, "Nathan's here!"

Even though Blaze understood that Nathan's mom and dad were here too, it was Nathan who got the big announcement.

And I think something similar is at work in the gospel stories about Jesus.

WHEN WE TELL THE STORY OF JESUS' LIFE, DEATH, RESURrection, and ascension, in a magnificent yet down-to-earth way, we are telling the story of Father, Son, and Holy Spirit.

Let me put that another way:

The Holy Spirit reveals the Father to us through the life of the Son.

"My father gave me everything," Jesus said. "Nobody knows the son except the father, and nobody knows the father except the son—and anyone the son wants to reveal him to" (Matt. 11:27).

What Jesus is getting at here—and it's so important for us to understand—is that nobody knows what God is truly like unless we see God through Jesus, the Son. "He is the image of God," explains Paul in Colossians, "the invisible one . . . for in him all the Fullness was glad to dwell" (1:15–19).

All the glory of God in creation,
all the wisdom of God in scripture—
all of it still falls short in comparison with Jesus.

Because Jesus, remember, "is the shining reflection of God's own glory, the precise expression of his own very being . . ." (Heb. 1:3).

That's why all of our theology,
all of our God musings and doings—

all of it must finally be shaped by the image of God we see in the person of Jesus.

And that's very good news, isn't it? Like my son, Blaze, it makes me want to shout aloud for the whole world to hear, "Jesus is here!"

In the memorable words of British writer and composer Anthony Burgess, "If God is like Jesus, God is worth believing in."[57]

In fact, just after Jesus explains this like-Father-like-Son image that is uniquely reflected in him, and as if Jesus is anticipating our fears and objections to the various and confusing ideas about God that are so often forced on us, Jesus goes on to say:

> "Are you tired? Worn out? Burned out on religion? Come to me. Get away with me and you'll recover your life. I'll show you how to take a real rest. Walk with me and work with me—watch how I do it. *Learn the unforced rhythms of grace.* I won't lay anything heavy or ill-fitting on you. Keep company with me and you'll learn to live freely and lightly." (Matt. 11:28–30 *The Message*, italics added)

"The unforced rhythms of grace"—"freely and lightly" in step with King Jesus: Now isn't that the sort of Jesus journey that you and I and the whole world need?

But the journey is only just beginning.

WHEN KING JESUS ASCENDED TO THE FATHER, HE DID NOT leave us alone. Jesus sent the Holy Spirit to be with us—even *in* us!—as we eagerly await the return of the King.

"I will ask the father," Jesus says in John 14:16, "and he will give you another helper, to be with you forever . . ."

> "I've said all this to you while I'm here with you. But the helper, the holy spirit, the one the father will send in my name . . . will teach

you everything. [And] bring back to your mind everything I've said to you." (John 14:25–26)

So what exactly does the Holy Spirit do in you and me?

For starters, the Holy Spirit helps us see and experience King Jesus of the gospel: the love and power, conviction and forgiveness, healing and wholeness that come only in him. If you have experienced some of that in these pages, if your heart, in the famous words of John Wesley, has been "strangely warmed" in reading of Jesus' life, death, and resurrection, that's because Holy Spirit has been with you—and that's amazing.

But the work of the Holy Spirit does not stop there.

According to the apostle Paul, "the love of God has been poured out in our hearts through the holy spirit" (Rom. 5:5), and we can now call God "Abba Father" just like Jesus did. "When that happens," Paul continues, "it is the spirit . . . giving supporting witness to what our own spirit is saying, that we are God's children" (Rom. 8:15–16).

If you have experienced in this book a new understanding of what it means that you are a child of God and that you have been forever welcomed, adopted into the family of God through King Jesus—the one who is and who always will be human—that's because the Holy Spirit is pouring the love of God into your heart, even now.

But the Holy Spirit is still not done.

Because the Holy Spirit intends to make us more and more like Jesus, "changed into the same image," in the words of 2 Corinthians 3:18, "from glory to glory." Please don't misunderstand what Paul is saying in this passage: the point is not to have a bunch of personality-free, indistinguishable Jesus clones obsessively asking themselves, "What would Jesus do? What would Jesus do?" (Even though that question, of course, is a good one to ask.)

And neither is the point that humans will, in effect, somehow become divine in the way that the Father, Son, and Holy Spirit are divine.

The Father's point, his plan, his eternal purpose is to have Spirit-alive people living and loving like Jesus throughout the whole earth, in every sphere of society and area of culture: carpenters and consultants, teachers and doctors, mechanics and zoologists, moms and dads, sons and daughters—all of us being "shaped according to . . . the image of his son, so that he might be the firstborn of a large family" (Rom. 8:29).

Jesus didn't come to make you less human. He came to make you more human, like him.

And the Holy Spirit is here to help you,
now and forever, in that Jesus journey:
Godspeed.

So: to the one who is capable of doing far, far more than we can ask or imagine, granted the power which is working in us—to him be glory, in the church, and in King Jesus, to all generations, and to the ages of ages! Amen! (Eph. 3:20–21)

ACKNOWLEDGMENTS

Like so many meaningful things, this book was conceived in conversation: In early morning, coffee-fueled chats with my best friend and wife, Bronwyn. In living room discussions with our East Boston church family, Ekklesia Eastie. In an ongoing, invigorating dialogue with teacher and friend Maureen Menard.

Also, I am grateful to my friend Aaron Reeves (tektonmaps.com) for a perfectly timed email. To Willard Cook, Dick Kiernan, Lisa Oelerich, and the board of Alpha New England for how they champion Jesus work on the campuses of New England and beyond (alpha.org). To Tom and Lyn Shields, Mike and Maura Glynn, and Caleb and Bonny Loring for their big-hearted generosity, and to Bonny and Caleb in particular for opening their home to me for a few focused days of writing. To the small collective of friends and family who help us do what we do in East Boston and beyond. To the Imago Dei Fund for enabling me to develop and teach the Jesus Series in partnership with student groups at MIT, Boston University, Emerson College, Tufts University, Merrimack College, and in multiple other young adult settings. To the global tribe called YWAM, my family in ministry for years, and to hundreds of YWAM Discipleship Training School students and staff with whom I've learned so much about Jesus in various teaching sessions around the world (ywam.org).

I have the rare blessing of being surrounded by a cadre of close brothers in faith upon whom I can always call for prayer and perspective, courage and conviction: Kurimay and Baumann (Godspeed in your healing, dear friend); all of the gentle beasts of Ekklesia—Roberto (for the steadying effect of floating church), Matthew, Bryan, J. Justin, Holt, Davis, Mr. Simons, Trimble, and in particular the Jordanian (who showed up unexpectedly on the most challenging day of writing); Beirut-Chud, Johannesburg-Joel, and Navah-Adam; Léon-Luke and J. Lohnes (not least for your insight into the writing ways of Jesus); the mysterious coconspirators of the ____lings; Bowers, J. Singlehurst, and P. Powell (I still have your copy of *The Challenge of Jesus*); and, of course, my irreplaceable brothers in blood, law, and love, Mark-ravius and Tré (aka Lenny), with whom I've had more conversations about Jesus than I can count.

The team at Zondervan has been outstanding, and I am particularly grateful to my main editor, Stephanie Smith, and to my production editor, Brian Phipps. While any remaining mistakes in writing and theology are mine, this book is undoubtedly stronger because of them.

Family is one of God's greatest gifts, and I could not be more thankful for my parents, Glenn and Jacquelyn Sheppard in Greenwood, Missouri (my mother is one of my best editors, and she carefully read this entire manuscript while busily attending to the release of her own book, *Silent Takeover*, an important and deeply insightful read about overcoming emotional, mental, and addictive disorders); Tré, Tori, Aidan, and Elena in Coleraine, Northern Ireland; Krista, Mark, Arianna, Hudson, and Hunter in Lee's Summit, Missouri; Mom Bonnie and Joellah in Izmir, Turkey, and Bonnie Rachel in Boston, Massachusetts. (BR, you offered such wise and insightful feedback along the way.)

Finally, to Bronwyn and our three children, Miréa, Blaze, and Petra: for your love and laughter, patience and peace, but most of all, Bronwyn, for your song—thank you. *Sizi seviyorum.*

NOTES

1. When it comes to understanding Jesus in his first-century setting, there is no better guide than N. T. Wright. A good place to begin is *Simply Jesus: A New Vision of Who He Was, What He Did, and Why He Matters* (New York: HarperOne, 2011). Jacob Neusner is one of the most prolific authors in history, and his *A Rabbi Talks with Jesus* (Montreal and Kingston: McGill-Queen's University Press, 2000) is a contemporary classic in Jewish and Christian dialogue. "In these pages," Neusner writes, "I treat Jesus with respect, but I also mean to argue with him about things he says." Finally, Anne Rice has written two pieces of historical fiction about the early years of Jesus, *Christ the Lord: Out of Egypt* (New York: Ballantine, 2008) and *Christ the Lord: The Road to Cana* (New York: Anchor, 2009). Although I don't believe the *Infancy Gospel of Thomas* is an accurate picture of Jesus' early life, I was nonetheless moved by Rice's beautiful and believable portrait of our Lord.

2. One of the reasons I have chosen to use N. T. Wright's and Eugene Peterson's translations is because both of these scholars have written popular and insightful books that explore how they approach the Bible. How one approaches the Bible, of course, shapes the way one translates the scriptures. For more, see N. T. Wright, *Scripture and the Authority of God: How to Read the Bible Today* (New York: HarperOne, 2013), and Eugene Peterson, *Eat This Book: A Conversation in the Art of Spiritual Reading* (Grand Rapids: Eerdmans, 2006). Also, see Wright's "Preface" in *The Kingdom New Testament: A Contemporary Translation* (New York: HarperOne, 2011), xi–xvii, and Peterson's "Introduction to the New Testament" in *The Message: New Testament with Psalms and Proverbs* (Colorado Springs: NavPress, 1993), 8–10.

3. N. T. Wright, *The Challenge of Jesus* (London: SPCK, 2000), 92.

4. Richard Mouw, an American theologian and philosopher, said something like this when he delivered the commencement address at the completion of my graduate studies at Wheaton College.

5. John Ortberg, *Who Is This Man?* (Grand Rapids: Zondervan, 2012), 21.

6. It was Eastie friend and coconspirator Matthew Neave who taught me to add "some" to this Christmas classic.

7. Gary Wills, *What Jesus Meant* (New York: Penguin, 2006), 3.

8. Thomas F. Torrance, *Incarnation: The Person and Life of Christ* (Downers Grove, IL: InterVarsity, 2008), 64, 106.

9. For more on this, see C. Baxter Kruger, *The Great Dance: The Christian Vision Revisited* (Vancouver: Regent College Publishing, 2000), 41–42. It is worth noting that Kruger did his doctoral dissertation on Professor Torrance's theology, and he studied under Torrance's brother, James.

10. Also, see my friend Pete Greig's riveting books *Red Moon Rising: How 24-7 Prayer Is Awakening a Generation* (Lake Mary, FL: Relevant, 2003) and *Dirty Glory: Go Where Your Best Prayers Take You* (Colorado Springs: NavPress, 2016) that chronicle the story of the 24-7 Prayer movement worldwide.

11. Chris Wright, *Knowing Jesus through the Old Testament* (London: Marshall Pickering, 1992), 108, italics added.

12. Samuel Smith, "Christian Man Dies Emulating Jesus' Forty-Day, Forty-Night Fast in the Wilderness," *The Christian Post*, August 13, 2015, www .christianpost.com/news/christian-man-dies-emulating-jesus-40-day-40 -night-fast-in-the-wilderness-142764/. Accessed August 1, 2016.

13. Relevant, "Diary of a Forty-Day Fast," *Relevant*, April 28, 2008, http:// ftp.relevantmagazine.com/god/deeper-walk/features/1452-diary-of-a-40 -day-fast. Accessed August 1, 2016.

14. These four examples are drawn from N. T. Wright, *How God Became King: The Forgotten Story of the Gospels* (New York: HarperOne, 2012), 95.

15. Robert H. Stein, *Jesus the Messiah: A Survey of the Life of Christ* (Downers Grove, IL: InterVarsity, 1996), 110, italics added.

16. Justin Welby, "A Personal Statement from the Archbishop of Canterbury," April 8, 2016, www.archbishopofcanterbury.org/articles.php/5704/a -personal-statement-from-the-archbishop-of-canterbury. Accessed April 11, 2016.

17. Jane Williams, "Statement by Jane Williams (Lady Williams of Elvel)," April 7, 2016, https://janewilliamsofelvel.com. Accessed April 11, 2016.

18. Charles Moore, "Winston Churchill's Right-hand Man and an Affair to Shake the Establishment," *The Telegraph*, April 8, 2016, www.telegraph.co .uk/news/2016/04/08/winston-churchills-right-hand-man-and-an-affair -to-shake-the-est/. Accessed April 11, 2016.

19. Tom Wright, *The Original Jesus: The Life and Vision of a Revolutionary* (Grand Rapids: Eerdmans, 1996), 29.

20. Bible teacher Ray Vander Laan is one of the most recent voices to

champion the idea of a young age for the disciples. For more, see Vander Laan's insightful article "Rabbi and Talmidim," www.thattheworldmay know.com/rabbi-and-talmidim. Accessed July 13, 2016.

21. Jacob Neusner, *Judaic Law from Jesus to the Mishnah* (Atlanta: Scholars Press, 1993), 77: "The Messiah would come when all Israel, through mastery of the Torah and obedience to it, had formed [the] holy community." Neusner says this in reference to post AD 70, but I believe it can be applied to Jesus' day as well.

22. Marcus J. Borg, *Conflict, Holiness, and Politics in the Teachings of Jesus* (Harrisburg, PA: Trinity Press International, 1998), 147.

23. Paula Fredriksen, *Jesus of Nazareth, King of the Jews* (New York: Vintage, 2000), 109: "The ill grab ahold of 'the fringe of his garment' (Mark 6:56); the term, *kraspedon* in Greek, translates the Hebrew *tzitzit*. These fringes are not decorative but ritual. God had instructed Moses on them in a passage in Numbers that was incorporated into the *Sh'ma*. 'Speak to the people of Israel and bid them to make tassels on the corners of their garments throughout their generations . . . to look upon and *to remember all the commandments of the Lord, to do them*' (Nm 15:38–39)."

24. Kenneth Bailey, *Jesus through Middle Eastern Eyes: Cultural Studies in the Gospels* (Downers Grove, IL: InterVarsity, 2008), 193.

25. Ibid.

26. Dorothy L. Sayers, *Are Women Human? Penetrating, Sensible, and Witty Essays on the Role of Women in Society* (Grand Rapids: Eerdmans, 1971), 46–47.

27. It was New Zealand teacher and friend Winkie Pratney who first pointed this out to me.

28. Ann Spangler and Lois Tverberg, *Sitting at the Feet of Rabbi Jesus: How the Jewishness of Jesus Can Transform Your Faith* (Grand Rapids: Zondervan, 2009), 51.

29. For an important and insightful discussion of what is and is not the kingdom, see Scot McKnight, *Kingdom Conspiracy: Returning to the Radical Mission of the Local Church* (Grand Rapids: Brazos, 2014).

30. Elton Trueblood, *The Humor of Christ* (New York: Harper and Row, 1964), 63.

31. Gareth Gilkeson, www.rendcollective.com/media, in the video *The Art of Celebration*. Accessed June 6, 2016. The music of Rend Collective, the Northern Irish band of which Gilkeson is a part, was a constant source of inspiration and encouragement throughout the writing of this book.

32. N. T. Wright, *Jesus and the Victory of God* (Minneapolis: Fortress, 1996), 423: "He was not attempting a reform [of Temple]; he was symbolizing judgment." I lean heavily into the work of Wright in this and the next chapter because I know of no other Jesus scholar who has so thoroughly and historically explored the nature of Jesus' understanding of the victory of the cross.

33. Grant R. Osborne, *Matthew: Exegetical Commentary on the New Testament* (Grand Rapids: Zondervan, 2010), 762.

34. Wright, *Simply Jesus*, 188: "The only way, he believed, by which this great anti-creation power could be stopped and defeated would be for him, Jesus, anointed with God's Spirit to fight the real battle against the real enemy, to take the full power of evil and its accusations upon himself, to let it do its worst to him, so that it would thereby be exhausted, its main force spent."

35. N. T. Wright, *Simply Christian* (London: SPCK, 2006), 94: "[Jesus] would be the place where God's future arrived in the present, with the kingdom of God celebrating its triumph over the kingdoms of this world by refusing to join in their spiral of violence. He would love his enemies. He would turn the other cheek. He would go the second mile. He would act out, finally, his own interpretation of the ancient prophecies which spoke, to him, of a suffering Messiah."

36. For more on this, see Caesar's coronation and procession compared with Jesus' coronation and procession in Shane Claiborne and Chris Haw, *Jesus for President* (Grand Rapids: Zondervan, 2008), 126–31.

37. For a simple introduction to a contemporary version of this ancient Jewish meal, see "The Seder Service in a Nutshell," www.chabad.org/holidays/passover/pesach_cdo/aid/1751/jewish/The-Seder-in-a-Nutshell.htm. Accessed August 3, 2016.

38. Wright, *Jesus and the Victory of God*, 609.

39. A fascinating and insightful introduction to Son of Man language and imagery in the first century and how Jesus may have applied the title to himself can be found in Rabbi Daniel Boyarin, *The Jewish Gospels: The Story of the Jewish Christ* (New York: The New Press, 2012). While I don't agree with all of Boyarin's conclusions, the first-century framework he provides for the title Son of Man is exceedingly helpful.

40. Richard John Neuhaus, *Death on a Friday Afternoon: Meditations on the Last Words of Jesus from the Cross* (New York: Basic Books, 2000), xii.

41. Quoted in David L. Bartlett and Barbara Brown Taylor, eds., *Feasting on*

the Word: Preaching the Revised Common Lectionary, year A, vol. 2, *Lent through Eastertide* (Louisville: Westminster John Knox, 2010), 312.

42. As quoted in Philip Schaff, ed., and David Schaff, rev., *The Creeds of Christendom*, vol. 1 (Grand Rapids: Baker, 1996), 21.

43. Bartlett and Taylor, *Feasting on the Word*, 312.

44. John Ortberg, *Who Is This Man?* (Grand Rapids: Zondervan, 2012), 185: "If you can find this Jesus in a grave, if you can find him in death, if you can find him in hell, where can you *not* find him?"

45. Ortberg points to a commentary by Dale Bruner that translates this moment as "And look! Jesus met them and said, 'Hi!'" As quoted in *Who Is This Man?* 187.

46. Robert J. Hutchinson, *Searching for Jesus: New Discoveries in the Quest for Jesus of Nazareth—and How They Confirm the Gospel Accounts* (Nashville: Thomas Nelson, 2015), 18.

47. I am grateful to my brother, Tré, for this vivid example of how the "truth" of an event can be remembered in different ways.

48. Géza Vermes, *Jesus the Jew: A Historian's Reading of the Gospel* (Philadelphia: Fortress, 1981), 41.

49. N. T. Wright, *Surprised by Hope: Rethinking Heaven, the Resurrection and the Mission of the Church* (New York: HarperOne, 2008), 261.

50. I believe it was from Winkie Pratney that I first heard this memorable description of Jesus' resurrected body passing through locked doors "like you and I pass through the morning mist." Winkie was referring to C. S. Lewis's stunning description of heavenly-new-earth-reality as experienced in Lewis's wonderful book *The Great Divorce* (New York: HarperOne, 1946).

51. C. S. Lewis, *Miracles* (London: Fontana, 1960), 126–27.

52. C. Baxter Kruger, *The Great Dance: The Christian Vision Revisited* (Vancouver: Regent College Publishing, 2000), 22.

53. Ibid., 36.

54. Ibid., 38.

55. C. Baxter Kruger, *Jesus and the Undoing of Adam* (Jackson: Perechoresis Press, 2003), 54–55.

56. C. S. Lewis, *Mere Christianity* (New York: Macmillan, 1952), 153, parentheses in original.

57. Quoted in Nicky Gumbel's "Bible in One Year," http://archive.htb.org.uk/one-year-bible/uniqueness-jesus-0. Accessed August 16, 2016.